Buddhist Cosmology

BUDDHIST COSMOLOGY
Philosophy and Origins

by
Akira Sadakata

translated by
Gaynor Sekimori

with a foreword by
Hajime Nakamura

KŌSEI PUBLISHING CO. • *Tokyo*

Shown on the cover is a painting entitled *Hasu no Hikari* (Lotus Light) by Josaku Maeda.

Editing by Joy S. Sobeck. Cover design and layout of photographs by NOBU. The text of this book is set in Monotype Baskerville with a computer version of Optima for display.

First English edition, 1997

Published by Kōsei Publishing Co., 2-7-1 Wada, Suginami-ku, Tokyo 166.
 Printed in Japan.

ISBN 4-333-01682-7 LCC Card No. applied for

Contents

Figures

Foreword

Buddhist cosmology is highly complicated compared to that of the Vedas, and much more advanced in its use of extraordinary numbers. When we read in the scriptures the complex numerical descriptions of the Buddhist universe, we feel overwhelmed. Even specialists find it difficult to understand the structure of Buddhist cosmology.

Thus few scholars have tried to explain the Buddhist view of the universe. One exception is William Montgomery McGovern, in his *A Manual of Buddhist Philosophy,* vol. 1: Cosmology (London: Trübner, 1923). McGovern was well versed in the scholarship set forth in Chinese versions of Mahāyāna scriptures. Louis de la Vallée Poussin's article "Cosmogony and cosmology (Buddhist)" (*Encyclopaedia of Religion and Ethics,* vol. 4 [Edinburgh: T. & T. Clark, 1974 (1911)], pp. 129–38) is a sounder treatment of the theme, based on profound scholarship. Poussin's *Vasubandhu et Yaçomitra,* ch. 3 of *L'Abhidharmakoça Kārikā, Bhāṣya et Vyākhyā* (Bouddhisme: Études et materiaux—Cosmologie; le monde des êtres et le monde-réceptacle, tome 6 [Bruxelles: Académie Royale de Belgique, 1919]) is an elaborate work and displays the author's high scholarly standard, but its materials are limited in scope, so that it is not useful to laypersons.

Now, in Professor Sadakata's *Buddhist Cosmology,* we have a clear and accurate explanation of the subject. This work is based on his first book, *Shumisen to gokuraku* (Mount Sumeru and paradise), which revived a seemingly defunct Buddhist cosmology by viewing ancient themes from a modern perspective. His knowledge of European culture and his extensive travels to significant historical sites in South and Central Asia imbue this work with a cross-cultural and comparative perspective. *Buddhist Cosmology* brings many Buddhist sources to the attention of Western scholars for the first time. Even those who may disagree on minor points cannot disregard this pioneering work.

To today's reader, Buddhist teachings about the universe's structure may appear to be absurd. But Professor Sadakata finds many similarities between the cosmology of modern science and that of Buddhism. He also shows us how, even today, this ancient philosophy can help us lead more fulfilling lives. By clearly explaining difficult themes, Professor Sadakata has opened the door to Buddhist cosmology, and for that I am glad.

Hajime Nakamura
Professor Emeritus
The University of Tokyo

Preface

The teachings of Buddhism aim to lead people from the realm of delusion, the everyday world, to the realm of enlightenment. It is not surprising, therefore, that there should be large numbers of publications on the market explaining its practice, beliefs, and scriptures. To penetrate the realm of enlightenment, though, it is necessary to understand the realm of delusion. Likewise, explanation of the realm of delusion entails reference to the realm of enlightenment, and studies of Buddhist cosmological ideas are useful in this regard.

Such publications are surprisingly few; many years have passed since I sought to rectify the lack of such works by writing my *Shumisen to gokuraku* (Mount Sumeru and paradise). In *Buddhist Cosmology,* I focus on concrete and specific descriptions of cosmology rather than on abstract doctrines. It is my hope that this book will be accessible and interesting to laypeople.

I owe my thanks to a number of people who have been instrumental in bringing out this English translation. I would like first of all to acknowledge my gratitude to the translator, Gaynor Sekimori. A scholar of Buddhism, she has produced a lucid and accurate translation. My thanks go also to the book's editor, Joy S. Sobeck, whose professional expertise and rearrangement of the text have made the result extremely readable. The book also owes much to the efforts of the publisher, who amplified the text at essential points by adding supplementary information from my other books and essays, and identified the sources of the quotations. I can truly say that the translated version represents a great improvement on the original.

Finally, I would like to express my gratitude to my mentor, Professor Hajime Nakamura. In the midst of a very busy schedule he was kind enough to write the foreword to the English edition. It is a matter of great happiness and honor that he remains in good health and continues to show many kindnesses to me, his student for thirty-seven years.

Editorial Note

In this book, the plurals of the Sanskrit terms have been made in the English style, by adding *s* (for example, *yojanas*).

The names of premodern Japanese (for example, Hirata Atsutane) are given in the Japanese style, with the surname first, and those of modern (post-1868) Japanese (for example, Ryōun Kamegai) are given in the Western style, with the surname last.

PART ONE

Pre-Mahāyāna Cosmology

1. The Structure of Matter and the Universe

Buddhism's view of the universe has undergone many changes over the last 2,500 years. Very broadly, we can divide Buddhist cosmology into two streams, Abhidharma and Mahāyāna. About a hundred years after Śākyamuni's death in the fourth or fifth century B.C.E., Buddhism split into two schools, and in the following two or three hundred years these divided further into eighteen or twenty schools, which are collectively called Abhidharma Buddhism. Around the first century B.C.E. a movement to restore the original spirit of Buddhism arose in reaction to Abhidharma Buddhism, which had become formalized and academic. The reformers called their form of Buddhism *Mahāyāna* ("great vehicle") and labeled Abhidharma Buddhism *Hīnayāna* ("small or lesser vehicle"). Toward the end of the Mahāyāna period, esoteric or Tantric Buddhism made its appearance, and this form of Buddhism also had its distinctive view of the universe. In this book, though, I deal only with the Hīnayāna and Mahāyāna traditions.

Buddhist cosmology according to the Hīnayāna tradition centers on (1) the realm of Mount Sumeru, (2) *dharmas* (the Buddha's teachings), and (3) the notion that the Buddha (Śākyamuni) is a historical person. In Mahāyāna Buddhism, (1) the various "buddha-realms" are more prominent than Mount Sumeru, (2) the Buddha (or buddhas) takes precedence over dharmas, and (3) the Buddha is a suprahuman (cosmological) existence. As we shall see in part 2, Mahāyāna views thus changed Buddhism from a philosophy to a religion.

I have relied principally on Vasubandhu's *Abhidharmakośa* (Abhidharma storehouse treatise) for my description of pre-Mahāyāna cosmology which makes up part 1 of this book. This work, dating from the fifth century C.E., contains an excellent and concise description of the Buddhist view of the cosmos.[1] For my treatment of Mahāyāna cosmology in part 2, I have depended chiefly on the *Flower Garland Sūtra* (ca. 3d century C.E.) and the *Larger Sukhāvatī-vyūha* (ca. 2d century C.E.). Though the *Abhidharmakośa* dates from the fifth century, it inherits a doctrinal stance that predates the common era, so we can say that both the *Flower Garland Sūtra* and the *Larger Sukhāvatī-vyūha* actually postdate the *Abhidharmakośa* in terms of doctrinal development.

Basic Components of Matter

The smallest particles. Just as the modern scientific view of the cosmos is based on atomic theory, Buddhism posits elements and atoms along with its theory of the universe's structure. The fifth-century *Abhidharmakośa* examines elements and atoms in a chapter entitled "Analyzing the world (*dhātu*)." Let us look at how the *Abhidharmakośa* treats the subject and supplement the explanation using the *Great Commentary* (Abhidharma-mahā-vibhāṣā-śāstra, ca. 100–150 C.E.), an encyclopedia of the thought of the Sarvāstivādins (one of the twenty Hīnayāna schools), of which the *Abhidharmakośa* is a compendium.

These Buddhist texts discuss particles called atoms (*paramāṇus*), defined as "the smallest part of matter, uncuttable, unable to be destroyed, taken up, or grasped. They are neither long nor short, neither square nor round. They cannot be analyzed, seen, heard, or touched."[2] *Paramāṇu* derives from *parama* ("extreme") and *aṇu* ("minute"). This definition reminds us of the Greek *atomos* ("atom"), made up of *a* ("not") and *tomos* ("cut").

Paramāṇus cannot exist individually; only when many *paramāṇus* accumulate can they occupy space and undergo change.

According to the *Abhidharmakośa,* in the first step of this process, one of seven *paramāṇus* becomes the nucleus around which the other six spread themselves three-dimensionally, making one molecule (*aṇu;* see figure 1). However, according to the Vaiśeṣika school of thought (one of the six principal Brahmanical, or orthodox Hindu philosophies), matter becomes visible as follows. Two *paramāṇus* make a molecule, a particle called a *dvyaṇuka.* Three such *dvyaṇukas* join to make a *tryaṇuka,* which is the size of a *trasareṇu,* a dust mote visible in the rays of the sun. Four *tryaṇukas* make a *caturaṇuka* (see figure 2). Thus larger and larger particles form, eventually creating matter that we are able to perceive. This process occurs by means of the power of *adṛṣṭa,* "invisible force."

All matter is said to be made up of the "four great elements" (*catvāri mahā-bhūtāni*): earth, water, fire, and wind. Whereas the *paramāṇus* are matter, the four great elements seem to be energy. They are not the physical earth, water, fire, and wind that we see or feel around us; they are invisible, though they do occupy space. As energy, the four great elements constitute *paramāṇus,* and it is only when numbers of *paramāṇus* congregate that we are able to perceive earth, water, fire, or wind themselves, or any other matter that exists.

Each element has special characteristics and functions: earth is solid and supports things; water is moist and dissolves things; fire is hot and boils things; and wind is mobile and causes things

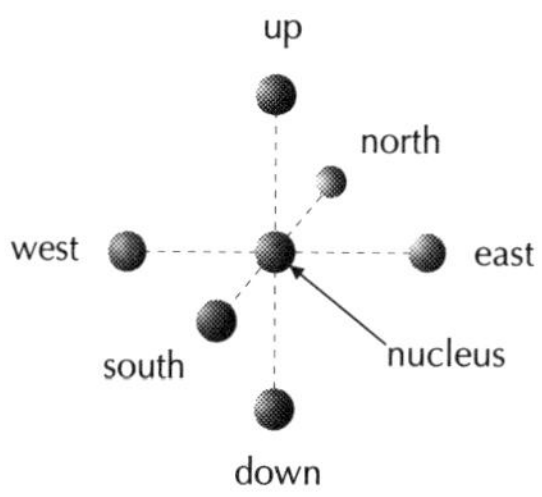

Fig. 1. Structure of a Molecule, according to the *Abhidharmakośa*

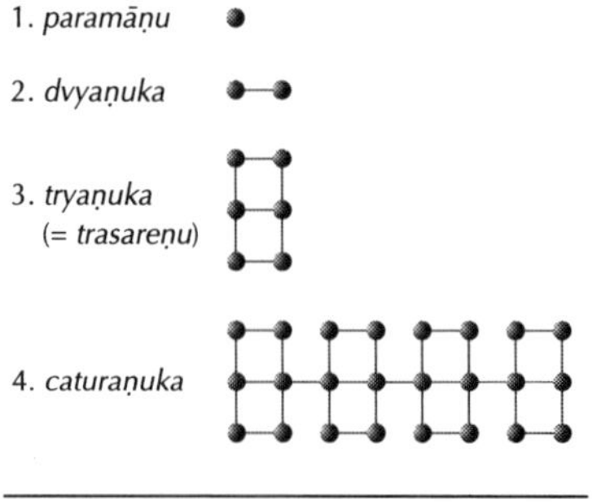

Fig. 2. Structure of Atoms and Molecules according to the Vaiśeṣika School

to grow. (Wind, consisting of air, was believed to be like breath, and therefore it was thought to cause growth or at least to maintain existence.) The elements do not exhibit their presence equally in all types of matter. Some particular elements are abundant in one thing; other elements are abundant in another thing. That is why some matter is solid, some pliant, some moist, and some hot. Another explanation has it that in any matter, the four elements are equally mixed and that only a particular element among them has the power to determine the characteristics of that matter.

Greek atomism. What is the origin of Indian atomic theory? According to Buddhist sources, the theory of the elements was expounded by Ajita Kesakambalin and Pakudha Kaccāyana, two philosophers who were active in India at the same time as Śākyamuni Buddha (ca. 560–ca. 480 B.C.E. or ca. 460–ca. 380 B.C.E.). Ajita taught that only the four elements—earth, water, fire, and wind—have true reality, being independent and immutable. Human beings are composed of these four elements, and when they die, the earth part of their composition returns to join the earth in the world, as do the water, fire, and wind parts to the water, fire, and wind in the world. The faculties of the various organs return to empty space. Pakudha taught the existence of seven elements, adding suffering, pleasure, and the life force to the above four. "There is neither the killer nor the killed. . . . Even if [someone] cuts off the head with a sharp sword, no one takes the life of any other [because] the sword only passes through the spaces of the seven elements."[3]

Several other Indian schools of philosophy also have such theories. For example, the Vaiśeṣika school, the oldest of the six orthodox Hindu philosophical systems, declares that atoms are not infinitely small, for if they were, both Mount Sumeru (the enormous mountain thought to be the center of the universe) and a mustard seed would be made up of an infinite number of atoms and therefore be of the same size.[4]

There is also a strong possibility that Greek philosophy influenced Indian atomic theories. In the fifth century B.C.E., Empedocles suggested that the four elements—water, air, fire, and earth—were the primary constituents of the universe, and Democritus posited the existence of atoms. Aristotle (384–22 B.C.E.) accepted the theory of the elements and assigned them particular characteristics (see figure 3).

It appears that, chronologically, the Indians were slightly in advance of the Greeks regarding the theory of the elements.

	Aristotle			Vaiśeṣika school		
Element	Sense	Movement	Tactile quality	Sense	Action	Tactile quality
earth	touch	downward	cold, dry	sight taste smell* touch	heaviness	neither hot nor cold
water	sight	stationary; in-between	cold, moist	sight taste* touch	heaviness	cold
fire	smell	upward	hot, dry	sight* touch	moves upward	hot
wind	hearing	stationary; in-between	hot, moist	touch*	moves horizontally	neither hot nor cold

Fig. 3. Comparison of Greek and Vaiśeṣika Theories of the Properties of the Elements
* indicates an element's most closely associated sense.

Still, the Buddhist sūtras were composed over a long span of time, and many new materials were added to the texts before they took their final written form. If we consider that the texts under discussion, and the Vaiśeṣika works as well, took their permanent form some time after the fourth century B.C.E., then the theory of the elements might very well have come to India from Greece. The many points of similarity between the Greek and Indian theories are obvious, as is an overall agreement despite some differences in individual items.

One final point illustrates the possible Greek origin of Buddhist atomic theories. A fifth element, space (*ākāśa*), was eventually added to Buddhism's four great elements. In esoteric Buddhism, the five great elements, like the five seed words, five shapes, and five bodily constituents, symbolized the essence of the universe, in a way analogous to the Chinese theory of five elements (*wu-hsing;* see figure 4). Democritus also wrote of space, not as a separate element, but as the location in which the four

Five great elements	Five shapes	Five bodily constituents	Five seed words	Tombstone	Wooden memorial tablet
space	almond	crown of head	𑖏 *kha* (unobstructed void)		
wind	crescent	brow	𑖮 *h(etva)* (origin)		
fire	triangle	chest	𑖨 *ra(ja)* (dust)		
water	sphere	navel	𑖪 *va(ktva)* (word)		
earth	square	knee	𑖀 *a(nutpāda)* (originally unborn)		

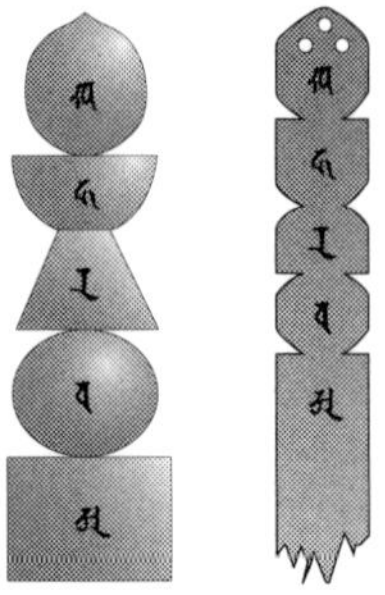

Fig. 4. Esoteric Buddhist Elements with Their Graphic Representations and Siddhaṃ (Ancient Indian) Characters

In Japan, a "five-stone-stūpa" (*gorintō*) tombstone formally represents the five great elements (*gorin*). When a person dies, he or she returns to the universe. Tombstones consisting of five stones of different shape, each representing one element, reflect the oneness of the human body with the universe. Those who could not afford to construct such tombstones made do with tall, upright wooden tablets bearing the five elements' symbols to mark the grave site.

elements acted. In the fact that the Buddhists actually made space a fifth element, and that it seems to be qualitatively the same as the other four, we can conjecture that they copied Greek philosophy but erred in interpretation. Later chapters in this book discuss other Greek influences on Indian thought, and routes and sites of cultural exchange.

The Universe

In Buddhism, the common Sanskrit term for "universe" is *loka-dhātu.* It refers to a place that has come into existence through the *karma* (actions and their enduring results) produced by living beings. The universe is also maintained by karma and disintegrates through the action of karma. In later Buddhism, beginning in the second or third century, it was believed that the *loka-dhātu* existed within the human mind. The term *universe* came to have such a strong connotation of human life and destiny that it almost ceased to connote the universe as a spatial entity.

The *Abhidharmakośa* describes the universe as follows. A circle of wind (*vāyumaṇḍala*) floats in space (*ākāśa*). This wind circle is disk-shaped, 10^{59} *yojanas* in circumference and 1,600,000 *yojanas* in depth. (There are various explanations concerning the length of a *yojana;* one says it is about seven kilometers.) Resting on the wind circle is a disk of water (*jalamaṇḍala*); it has a diameter of 1,203,450 *yojanas* and a depth of 800,000 *yojanas.* Above the water circle is a disk-shaped layer of golden earth (*kāñcanamaṇḍala*), of the same diameter and 320,000 *yojanas* in depth. Its upper surface supports mountains, seas, and islands. To visualize the composition more easily, imagine a basin (the water circle) placed on top of a washtub (the wind circle), with a birthday cake (the golden earth circle with mountains) surmounting it.

The diameters of the water and golden earth layers are the same, because these two layers were originally a single layer, or more correctly a cylinder, of water only. The golden earth layer was formed as skin forms on the surface of boiling milk. The borderline between the two layers is called the *golden ring extremity*, an expression which has come to mean "the bottom-most place." For humans, who live in one small section on top of the golden earth layer, the golden ring extremity is certainly the very bottom of the world.

Mount Sumeru. There are nine mountain ranges on the surface of the golden earth layer. Towering in the very center is Mount Sumeru, with seven ranges forming concentric squares around it. Proceeding outward, the seven ranges are called Yugandhara, Īṣādhāra, Khadiraka, Sudarśana, Aśvakarṇa, Vinataka, and Nimindhara.[5] Beyond Nimindhara are four landmasses, spoken of as islands or continents. They are named Pūrvavideha (from *pūrva,* "east") to the east of Sumeru, Aparagodānīya (from *apara,* "west") to the west, and Uttarakuru (from *uttara,* "north") to the north. In the case of Jambudvīpa, the southern landmass, the prefix *dakṣiṇa,* "south," is omitted. On the perimeter of the golden earth layer is a circular range of iron mountains called Cakravāḍa, which prevents the waters of the great sea containing the four landmasses from falling into the void. The other seven ranges are made of gold, and Sumeru, in the center, is made of the four treasures: gold on its northern face, silver on its eastern face, lapis lazuli on its southern face, and crystal on its western face. Because Jambudvīpa is south of Mount Sumeru, its sky is blue, reflecting the lapis lazuli of the southern face. The mountains and landmasses penetrate the waters (see figure 5).

Many traditional representations of Mount Sumeru portray the seven mountain ranges as arranged in concentric circles, but according to the *Abhidharmakośa,* they are squares, with sides of 80,000 *yojanas* each (see figure 6). A cross-sectional view shows the waters of the various seas as having a uniform depth of 80,000 *yojanas,* about 560,000 kilometers. This vastly surpasses the deepest known part of our oceans, the Mariana Trench, some 10 kilometers deep. Sumeru has a height of 160,000 *yojanas,* of

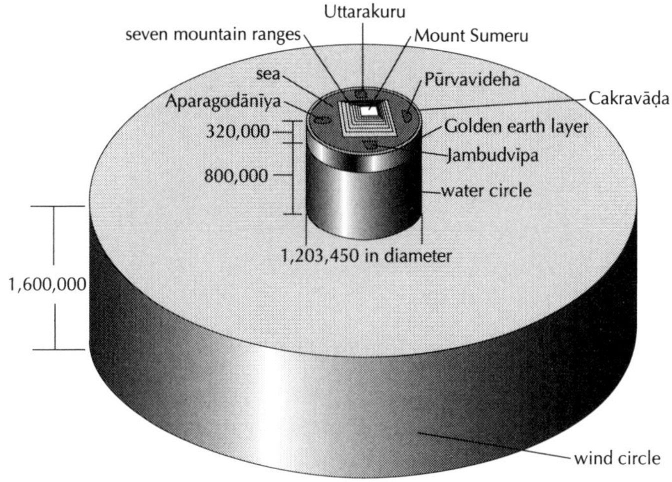

Fig. 5. Bird's-Eye View of the Mount Sumeru Realm
Dimensions are given in *yojanas*. (1 *yojana* is approximately 7 kilometers.)

which half is under water. The half above water is therefore 80,000 *yojanas* high. The heights above sea level of the eight ranges surrounding Sumeru are halved progressively from innermost to outermost.

So far, it has been easy to grasp the surface configuration of the golden earth layer. Two variables now complicate the matter. First, the width of each mountain range equals its height above sea level, which means that the width of each range is only half the width of the next range inward. Second, the widths of the seas also decrease progressively by half. The outermost sea, that between Nimindhara and Cakravāḍa, is very wide, however, as shown in figure 7.[6]

Mount Sumeru, with a height of some 560,000 kilometers, is far taller than the tallest mountain in the Himalayas. The name Sumeru (sometimes Śumeru) recalls Sumer (or Shumer), the center of an ancient Mesopotamian civilization. The similarity in names seems to be no more than a coincidence, however.

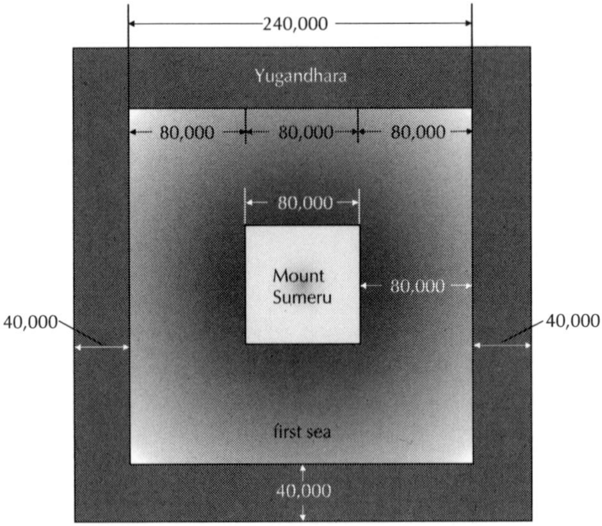

Fig. 6. Mount Sumeru as a Square
The *Abhidharmakośa* says, "The width of the first of the seven seas [that between Sumeru and Yugandhara] is 80,000 *yojanas.* The length [of the sea] is three times [80,000 *yojanas*]. When measuring [one of the four sides that are] the seashores of Yugandhara, it becomes 240,000 *yojanas*" (*Abhidharmakośa,* lines 13–15, *Taishō Tripiṭaka,* vol. 29, p. 57c). Cf. Leo M. Pruden, *Abhidharmakośabhāṣyam by Louis de la Vallée Poussin,* vol. 2 (Berkeley, Calif.: Asian Humanities Press, 1989), p. 454. (Dimensions are given in *yojanas.*)

The earliest appearance of the mountain's name in literature is in the *Mahābhārata,* the great Indian epic composed between the fourth century B.C.E. and the fourth century C.E., where it is called Meru. Buddhism no doubt adopted the name from that source. By adding the eulogistic Indo-Aryan prefix *su-* ("wonderful"), we get Sumeru.[7]

P. B. Spooner links Meru to Merv—not the town of Merv in Turkmeniya, but the Merv near Persepolis in Iran, a sacred mountain associated with the rise of the Achaemenid empire in the seventh century B.C.E. He also points out that the number thirty-three, in the heaven of the thirty-three gods on Sumeru's summit, is Zoroastrian, from Persia.[8] The invading forces of Alexander the Great (ca. 330 B.C.E.) heard the name *Melos*

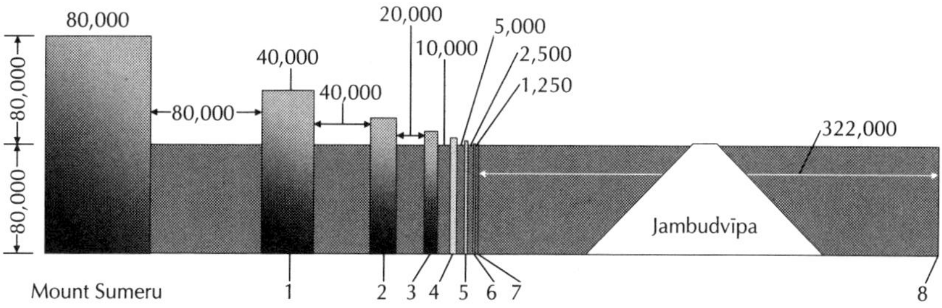

Fig. 7. Sizes of Mount Sumeru and Surrounding Mountains and Seas
1) Yugandhara (40,000); 2) Īṣādhāra (20,000); 3) Khadiraka (10,000); 4) Sudarśana (5,000); 5) Aśvakarṇa (2,500); 6) Vinataka (1,250); 7) Nimindhara (625); 8) Cakravāḍa (312.5). (Dimensions are given in *yojanas.*)

(*Merus*), and thought it had its origins in the thigh (*melos*) of Zeus.[9] In addition, there seems to be a lingering tradition or memory of life at higher latitudes when we consider that the sun, moon, and stars revolve on a horizontal plane around Mount Sumeru (see figure 8). This reminds us that one theory has the Indo-Aryans coming from the direction of Russia, and that the northern land of Uttarakuru was considered a utopia.[10]

All the same, there is a strong likelihood that the idea of the Mount Sumeru world originated not from geographical or historical reality but from the ancient Indian idea of a world axis. Mount Sumeru is the pillar that stands in the center of the world. When we add the wind layer below it and the heavens above it, we can see that this pillar penetrates the universe from top to bottom. The four directions are located with the pillar as center. The Indian liking for symmetry may have been a natural outgrowth of this concept of the directions.

P. Mus has argued that the *stūpa* (the dome-shaped Buddhist shrine) incorporates and expresses the Mount Sumeru world. The hemispherical dome (*aṇḍa*) covers the whole structure. The *cattrāvalī*, a series of parasols on the top, represents the various heavens of the realm of form, and the *harmikā*, the square pavilion surmounting the dome, represents the heaven of the thirty-three gods. The pole (*yaṣṭi*) fixed to the *harmikā* and supporting

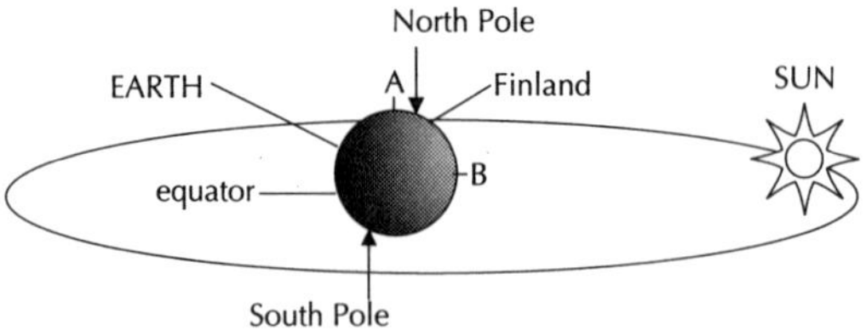

Fig. 8. Planet Revolution at High Latitudes
For a person at point A, the sun seems to revolve horizontally. For a person at point B, however, the sun appears to revolve perpendicular to the horizon. People living at higher latitudes—say, in Finland—might naturally believe that the planets revolve horizontally around the earth. If Indo-Aryans came from the direction of Russia, this belief may have influenced the Buddhist view that the planets revolved horizontally around Mount Sumeru.

the series of parasols is the world axis. The four gateways (*toraṇa*) on the north, south, east, and west sides of Stūpa 1 at Sāñcī, India (see photo 1 and figure 9) express the Indian idea of direction.[11] Archaeological investigations have revealed that this stūpa's foundation has the form of a spoked wheel (see figure 10). This may be no more than a simple structural feature, inasmuch as it was not visible once the stūpa had been completed. All the same, the idea of the world axis and the directions may have played a part in its adoption. The spoked wheel was also used to represent the Wheel of the Dharma, possibly derived from the spokes of a chariot wheel or the sun's disk, and also perhaps related to the concept of direction.[12]

The Indian subcontinent. Of the eight seas separating the mountain ranges, the inner seven are freshwater, but the vast outermost sea is of salt water. The four landmasses, each of different size and shape, are found in this large outer sea. Pūrvavideha, in the east, is shaped like a half-moon (though four sides are attributed to it). The curved side faces outward, and three sides measure 2,000 *yojanas* each whereas the fourth is only 350 *yojanas*. Jambudvīpa, in the south, is a trapezoid, the short side facing

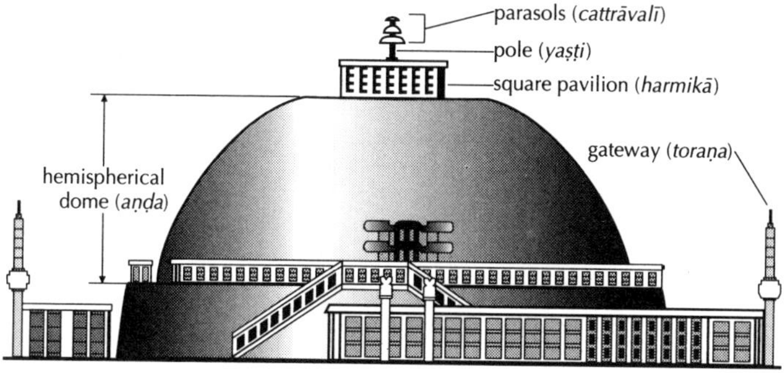

Fig. 9. Cross Section of Stūpa 1 at Sāñcī, Madhya Pradesh, India

outward. In fact, it is virtually a triangle. It has three sides of 2,000 *yojanas* each; the short side is 3.5 *yojanas*. Aparagodānīya, in the west, is a circle with a diameter of 2,500 *yojanas*. Uttarakuru, in the north, is a square, each side measuring 2,000 *yojanas*.

The southern land of Jambudvīpa is "our" world. Figure 11 makes it obvious that this continent's shape closely resembles the Indian subcontinent. Its various features bear this out; Jambudvīpa's characteristics correspond to the Indians' geographical knowledge. For instance, in the northern part is a mountain range called Himavat, "mountains of snow." These are the Himalayas (*hima,* "snow," and *ālaya,* "store").

Modern Indologists, finding that the *Abhidharmakośa* locates Lake Anavatapta ("no heat or fever") north of Himavat, searched for such a lake on existing maps. A clue to its location is that it was considered the common source of four great rivers, the Ganges, Indus, Oxus, and Śītā. Modern maps do not show these four rivers flowing from the same source. If, however, we extend the upper reaches of each of the four rivers, they would meet more or less where there actually is a large lake. This is Mānasarowar (Mapam in Tibetan), 4,602 meters above sea level, situated north of the Himalayas in modern Tibet. None of the four rivers mentioned flows from it, although the Sutlej, a tributary of the Indus, does. Near this lake is a mountain called

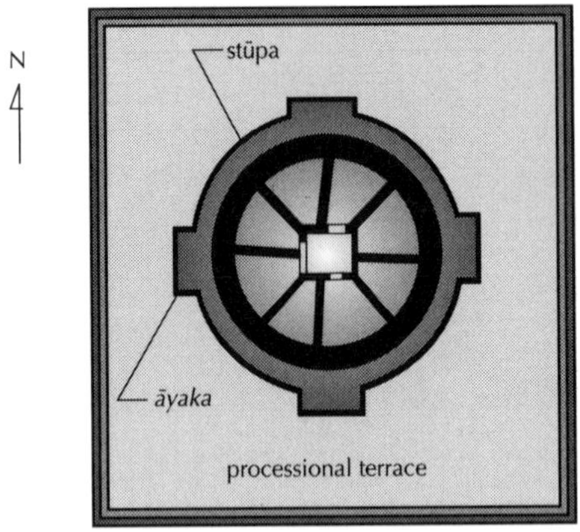

Fig. 10. Plan of Stūpa at Nāgārjunakoṇḍa, Andhrapradesh, South India
An *āyaka* is a base for monumental pillars.

Kailas, a pilgrimage site sacred both to Hindus and to Tibetan Buddhists. In view of the site's sacredness, perhaps we may be justified in conjecturing that Mānasarowar is indeed Anavatapta. Furthermore, Tibetan legend says that in ancient times the country had greater water resources than it does now and that its lakes were then very large. When they dried up they left smaller lakes dotted around the region. If these legends contain an element of truth, Mānasarowar could once have occupied a more extensive area than it does now and might very well have been the common source of the four rivers.

In any case, Anavatapta was a square, each side fifty *yojanas* long. According to the *Great Commentary*, the lake had four "mouths": in the east, the Ganges flowed from the mouth of a golden elephant; in the south, the Indus flowed from the mouth of a silver cow; in the west, the Oxus (Amu Darya) flowed from the mouth of a lapis lazuli horse; and in the north, the Śītā (possibly the modern Yarkand) flowed from the mouth of a crystal lion. What is interesting is that the rivers, on issuing from the lake, immediately made a circuit of the lake (whether clockwise or counterclockwise is not certain) before taking their true

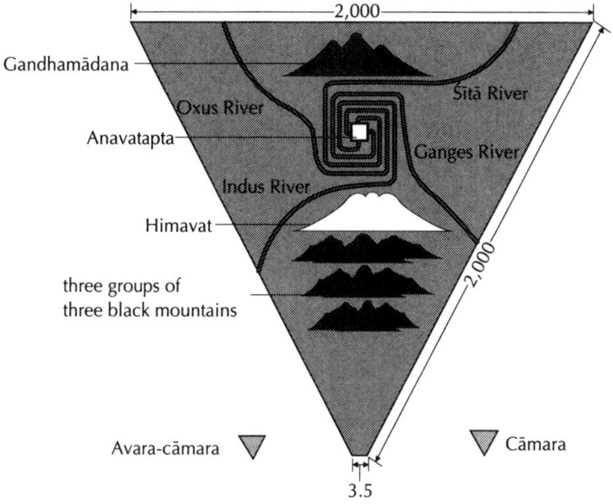

Fig. 11. Jambudvīpa according to the *Abhidharmakośa*
Dimensions are given in *yojanas.*

courses.[13] The depiction of the rivers as flowing from the mouths of animals probably stems from the same tradition as the spouts in the shape of lions' heads seen on jugs from the ancient Orient and Greece, on European fountains, and on water outlets in Japanese bathhouses.

Although the courses of the four great rivers are somewhat stylized, they still approximate actual geography. Moreover, the different materials and animals of the four outlets seem to depict the products of the regions in their corresponding directions. For example, in the south were gold and elephants. Gold was considered preeminent among the so-called four precious stones, and its placement in the south no doubt reflected the Indians' view of the importance of the South Asian continent. It is therefore of interest to see how this view of the world was treated by Buddhists who were not Indian.

Hsüan-tsang (600–664 C.E.), perhaps the best known of the Chinese priests who traveled to India, presents another diagram of the world, one that shows the four rulers of Jambudvīpa. In his diagram, the Elephant Lord appears in the south, the Jewel Lord in the west, the Horse Lord in the north, and the Lord of Human Beings in the east. This latter placement raised the status of the east by implying that the eastern land, clearly intended to be China, was where humanity and justice were practiced. The land of the Jewel Lord was the Near East, including Persia, where people valued wealth and possessions, and lacked propriety. The people in the north, in the domain of the Horse Lord, were wild and undisciplined. The land of the south should have been the superior one for a Buddhist, but Hsüan-tsang said that in etiquette and law the east was superior, whereas in religion the south was superior. Incidentally, Hsüan-tsang identified the Śītā River as the Yellow River; after disappearing into the desert sands in western China the Śītā reappeared further east as the Yellow.

Let us return to Anavatapta for a moment. Why it is called the "lake of no heat or fever" is unknown, although water on the plateau north of the Himalayas should certainly not be hot. For people living in a land of fiery heat, like India, absence of the affliction of heat was a condition of utopia and an indispensable element of a sacred realm. In Kirgiziya (Kirgizstan), just inside the border with China, there is a lake called Issyk-Kul, which means "hot lake." The area around this lake, which is 1,609 meters above sea level, is said to have a moderate climate, thanks to the water of the lake. From this we can conjecture that a lake of "*no* heat or fever" might be one with no warming influence on its surroundings, or, to interpret it more positively, a lake that ameliorates heat. Later, it came to be thought that a dragon lord of the same name lived in Anavatapta.

Y. Iwamoto compared Anavatapta and its four rivers with the Garden of Eden and its four rivers. He suggested that Anavatapta, as its name implies, is a mythologization of a desert oasis. The four rivers issuing from it correspond to the four rivers that flowed out of Eden, the Pishon, Gihon, Hiddekel (Tigris), and Phrat (Euphrates). Brahmanical works predating Buddhism tell the same legend of the flood contained in the Old Testament, and thus Iwamoto believes there is very likely a connection between Anavatapta and the Garden of Eden.[14]

Beside Anavatapta grow tall trees called jambu trees, whose fruit is said to be very sweet; the name of Jambudvīpa originates in that of the tree. North of the lake is the mountain Gandhamādana, "mountain of intoxicating fragrance." According to the *Sūtra on the Original Cause of the Origin of the World* (Ch'i-shih-yin-pen-ching; Dharmagupta's Chinese translation [ca. 600 C.E.] of the fourth part of the *Long Discourses* [Dīrghāgama]), many kinds of tree grow on the mountain, each emitting its own fragrance. Here live the *gandharvas,* demigods that serve Indra as musicians. They survive by eating fragrance (*gandha*). Under their control are innumerable *kiṃnaras,* performers of music and dance. Therefore on this mountain the sound of music is always heard.

Perhaps we could identify this mountain with Kailas (Ti-se in Tibetan). The name of Kailāsa appears in the *Mahābhārata,* where it is called the paradise of Śiva and as such later became a pilgrimage site for Hindus and later, Tibetans, followers of the Bon religion, as well as Buddhists. It appears that followers of Bon were the first to regard this mountain as sacred and contended with the Buddhists, who came later, concerning its possession.

South of Himavat are three groups of three black mountains. It is tempting to identify these with the Deccan Plateau, but they should more properly be considered the foothills of the Himalayas. Mochizuki's Buddhist dictionary defines Himavat as follows: "The three groups of black mountains would seem to indicate the ranges in the central part of the Himalayas, which grow taller from south to north. These ranges are the Sub-Himālaya, the Lower Himālaya, and the Snow Himālaya."[15]

It is rather strange to count the Snow Himālaya as one of the groups of black mountains, since "black" signifies a lack of snow. Nevertheless, the black mountains do seem to refer to Himalayan ranges. The photograph in Mochizuki's dictionary, showing the Himalayas from Darjeeling, shows clearly the contrast between the three groups of black mountains and the snow-covered mountains beyond.

South of Jambudvīpa are two islands, on either side of the lower tip of land. They are called Cāmara and Avara-cāmara. The island on the east is without a doubt Sri Lanka. West of India's southern tip are the Laccadives and the Maldives, but they are far smaller than Sri Lanka. The Indians, though, demanded symmetry and conformity, even to the extent of ignoring reality. By the same token, if there were two islands under Jambudvīpa, there had to be two islands under the other land masses as well. On either side of Pūrvavideha are Deha and Videha, Uttarakuru has its Kuru and Kaurava, and flanking Aparagodānīya are Śāṭha and Uttara-mantrin.

The Indians maintained this unreal view of the world even into the present millennium. In Greece, the geographer Ptolemy (Claudius Ptolemaeus, fl. 127–51 C.E.) knew that the world was round and made a world map employing lines of latitude and longitude. But in India, the fifth-century *Abhidharmakośa*'s cosmology was ethnocentric: "our" world, Jambudvīpa, was shaped like India. Central to any Indian worldview were the commanding, everpresent Himalayas. In Jambudvīpa these became the Himavat, the Mountains of Snow, as well as Mount Sumeru itself, on top of the golden earth layer.

The ancient Indians placed the four landmasses to the north, south, east, and west, and thought that their positions were unalterable for as long as the present *kalpa* lasted (a *kalpa* is an incalculably long period of time). Our knowledge of continental drift, however, tells us that this is not possible. We know, through examining the directional flow of terrestrial magnetism and the distribution of geological forms, which allows us theoretically to fit continents together, that the Indian subcontinent was once located near the South Pole, connected with Antarctica, Africa, and Australia.

The triangular Indian subcontinent split off from Antarctica ages ago and moved at a snail's pace until it hit against the floor of the Himalayas on the Asian continent. The impact pushed up the edge of Asia, forming the Himalayas. For some time there remained a gap between the two continents, into which sea water flowed. Over millions of years, sand from the Himalayas filled this gap, forming a layer of sand that at Varanasi is six thousand meters deep. Water flowing down from the mountains formed a river, as indicated in figure 12. The upper course

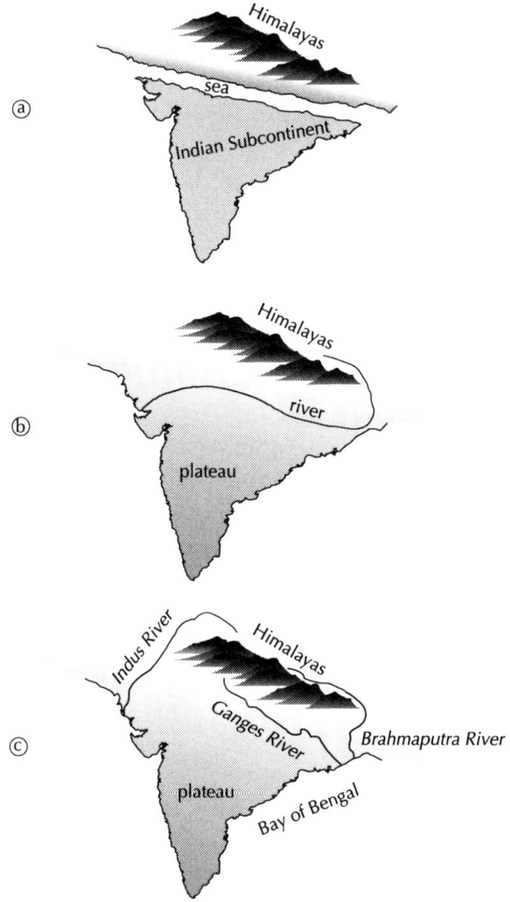

Fig. 12. Structural Changes in the Indian Subcontinent

of the river formed the present Brahmaputra, its middle course, the Ganges (flowing in a direction opposite to its present course), and its lower course, the Indus. At some point a great subsidence occurred in the area of Bengal. The river then flowed from that area into the sea and became divided into two rivers, the present Brahmaputra and the Ganges, which changed direction and gathered its waters from a different source. As a result of the Ganges' shift in direction, the Indus became a separate river. Of course the ancient Indians knew nothing of all this (as we also knew nothing until recently), for the subcontinent had changed position millions of years before human beings appeared, and the sinking of the Bengal area belongs to prehistory.

Sun and moon. The sun and the moon are components of any cosmology.[16] Imagine that a large ring of wind (like an inner tube) extends around Mount Sumeru at a height midway between mountaintop and sea level. This wind ring floats high in the air over the four landmasses, supporting and carrying the sun, moon, and stars. The sun is fifty-one *yojanas* in diameter and the moon, fifty, which makes them about the same size as Lake Anavatapta, north of the Himavat. To judge by the one-*yojana* difference, Indian Buddhists understood the apparent difference in size between the two bodies to be real. The stars are of varying sizes, the smallest being one *krośa* in diameter (less than a kilometer). The sun and moon do not themselves float in the ring of wind, but are contained within vehicles or receptacles called *vimāna*, "heavenly palace." The underside of the *vimāna* forms a circle of fire-pearl (ruby) to make the sun, and a circle of water-pearl to make the moon. Thus the sun shines brightly and is hot, whereas the moon gleams coldly. (The ancient Indians do not seem to have considered that the moon reflects the light of the sun.)[17]

One sun and one moon circle above the four landmasses. When the sun is over Jambudvīpa in the south, it is sunset in the eastern Pūrvavideha, sunrise in the western Aparagodānīya, and night in the northern Uttarakuru. Why do the lengths of days and nights change in the course of a year? According to the ancient Indians, the reason is that the sun moves continuously between north and south over Jambudvīpa. The *Abhidharmakośa* says, "When the sun moves to the southern part of Jambudvīpa [*dakṣiṇāyana*], the nights grow longer, and when it moves north [*uttarāyana*], the days grow longer."[18] This analysis is faulty. It is true that the sun continuously moves between north and south. This movement, however, does not explain the changes in the lengths of day and night; for this, knowledge of the earth's roundness is indispensable. Jambudvīpa, however, is on a plane surface.

There is also a problem with the sun's northward movement over Jambudvīpa. The Tropic of Cancer runs through the middle of India (see figure 13). A person living south of the Tropic, say in Hyderabad, would be able to confirm that the sun did move to the north. A sharp-eyed observer living in Delhi, north of the Tropic, however, would be sure to realize that the sun certainly did not pass over his head, that it was not true that "the sun moves to the north of Jambudvīpa." Megasthenes (ca. 3d century B.C.E.), the Greek (Seleucid) ambassador to the Mauryan court at Pātaliputra in the Ganges plain, was one such careful observer. He recorded that in certain places in India, shadows at certain times fell to the south, a strange phenomenon to a Greek who had lived only north of the Tropic of Cancer.

What causes the waxing and waning of the moon? "When the house of the moon moves in the vicinity of the house of the sun, then the light of the sun falls on the house of the moon. Consequently, the shadow falls on the opposite side, and the disk appears incomplete."[19] This seems to be a scientific explanation. The moon moves on a circular orbit (the wind ring), as does the sun. If the sun approaches the moon, the shadowed side of the moon should also move. But this is not a sufficient explanation, and the *Abhidharmakośa* therefore mentions the "manner of revolution"(*vāha-yoga*).[20] According to the commentaries, this appears

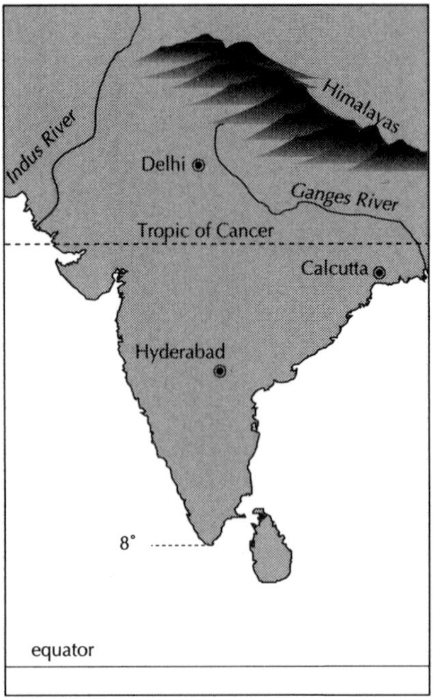

Fig. 13. Tropic of Cancer as It Passes over India

to mean that there is a difference in the heights of the sun's and moon's orbits. If the sun's orbit is higher than the moon's, it becomes much easier to explain the waxing and waning of the moon.

2. Hells, Heavens, and Other Realms

So far we have described the pre-Mahāyāna view of the secular world. In this chapter, we will discuss the sacred world according to pre-Mahāyāna philosophy.

Buddhism divides living beings into five types: gods (*deva*), human beings (*manuṣya*), animals (*tiryañc*), spirits of the dead (*preta*), and inhabitants of the hells (*naraka*). Sometimes a sixth type, demonic gods (*asura*), is added. These states of existence, among which living beings transmigrate (are reborn) depending on their karma, are called the five or six paths (see figure 14).

All living beings reside within the "realm of desire" (*kāma-dhātu*). Human beings and animals live together on the surface of the Mount Sumeru realm. Spirits and demonic gods live 500 *yojanas* under the earth, and the inhabitants of the hells, even deeper. Gods of various types live in the upper places, in the realm of form (*rūpa-dhātu*) and beyond that, in the realm of formlessness (*ārūpya-dhātu*). The realms of desire, form, and formlessness are known collectively as the "three realms" (*tri-dhātu*), in other words, the three kinds of worlds in which living beings exist. *Tri-dhātu* is a synonym for the universe as a whole, or for all existence.

Hells

Most religious cosmologies include the existence of hells somewhere in the universe, and Buddhism is no exception. "Hell" is

devas	superior	good paths
humans	ordinary	
asuras	inferior	
animals	superior	bad paths
hungry spirits	ordinary	
inhabitants of hells	inferior	

Fig. 14. The Six Paths of Transmigration

a translation of the Indic word *naraka* (or *niraya*), "devoid of happiness."[1] The hells are mentioned in a large number of Buddhist sūtras, either as a single entity, as in the *Verses on the Law* (Dhammapada, 4th–3d century B.C.E.), or as a system of individually named hells, as in the Abhidharma commentaries (very early Buddhist writings). They were certainly not systematized into an elaborate structure such as we see in the *Abhidharmakośa* for a very long time. There are also variations in the type and size of the hells in the various sūtras and commentaries, for the system of hells did not emerge as a single, comprehensive concept. It is the result rather of the ideas of scholar-priests over centuries, and because it belongs to the common intellectual heritage of all Indians, similar lists of hells exist in both Jainism and Hinduism.

The word *niraya* appears six times in the *Verses on the Law,* one of the earliest Buddhist texts we possess, where it is used simply to mean the destination of those who do evil. For example: "Some people are born on this earth; those who do evil are reborn in hell; the righteous go to heaven; but those who are pure reach nirvana" (126).[2] An equally old text, the *Group of Discourses* (Sutta-nipāta, written after the 3d century B.C.E.), also mentions hell in the same way. "Injuring someone with developed self, overwhelmed by ignorance, he does not know that defilement (is) the road which leads to hell" (277).[3]

The "Kokāliya" (or the Kokāliya-sutta) in the same work tells how the monk Kokāliya was reborn in the Paduma hell (*padumaniraya,* "red lotus hell") for censuring the teachers Sāriputta and Moggallāna, and then describes the horrors of this hell, warning that those who malign teachers of the Way will "go to hell for one hundred thousand and thirty-six Nirabuddas and five Abbudas [very long periods of time]" (660).[4] Verses 667–75 graphically describe the punishments of the hells (e.g., trees as sharp as blades, iron stakes, and a ball of heated iron), and their denizens (black and spotted dogs, ravens, and worms), which recall similar passages in the *Abhidharmakośa.*

A further point of interest is the list of ten hells in the "Kokāliya": Abbuda, Nirabudda, Abaha, Ahaha, Aṭaṭa, Kumuda, Sogandhika, Uppalaka, Puṇḍarīka, and Paduma. There is no reference in the *Group of Discourses* or in its commentary, *The Illustrator of Ultimate Meaning* (Paramatthajotikā, usually called Pj II; 5th century C.E.), to the origins of these names. Later commentators attempted to rationalize the names as denoting skin abscesses caused by cold (e.g., *abbuda*), or as onomatopoeic words to describe the cold of those hells (*abaha, ahaha, aṭaṭa*). The *Group of Discourses,* though, makes no mention of cold. The nineteenth sūtra in the *Long Discourses* and the *Commentary on the Great Perfection of Wisdom Sūtra* (Mahāprajñāpāramitā-upadeśa; 2d–3d century C.E.) say that the names denote the color of the hell and its walls (e.g., *uppalaka,* "blue lotus"; *paduma,* "red lotus").

The Pali Text Society edition of the *Pāli-English Dictionary* notes that the words *abbuda* and *nirabudda* denote extremely large numbers. *The Illustrator of Ultimate Meaning* offers the same interpretation, explaining that the Abbuda hell does not refer to a special hell as such, but to the amount of time (*abbuda*) that inmates are burned in the Avīci hell, the largest and lowest of the hot hells. The other designations are multiples of that unit. The word *nirabudda* appears in the *Jātakas* (tale no. 405, Bakabrahmajātaka; ca. 3d century B.C.E.?), tales of the Buddha's former lives, in a context unrelated to a hell, and the *Great Dictionary of the Meaning of Buddhist Terms* (Mahāvyutpatti, ca. 9th century), says that *utpala* and *padma* in Sanskrit (*uppalaka* and *paduma* in Pāli) both denote large numbers.[5] My own inclination, too, is to regard all of the names as signifying units of time. It is fair to say, then, that in the *Group of Discourses* (compiled after the 3d century B.C.E.) the system of multiple hells had not yet been devised.

Indian origins of the Buddhist concept of hell. The Indian epic, the *Mahābhārata* (4th century B.C.E.–4th century C.E.), describes hell in its final section. Yudhiṣṭhira, the eldest of the five Pāṇḍava brothers, is enabled by the powers of Indra to see hell and there to discover his brothers and his wife.[6] Hell is "shrouded in darkness," and it contains a large bird with an iron beak (perhaps a vulture), a copper pot, a tree whose branches are like blades, and the difficult-to-cross Vaitaraṇī River. The description is very close to that in the *Group of Discourses* (667–75).[7] The Brahmanic (orthodox Hindu) *Laws of Manu* (Manu-smṛti, 2d century B.C.E.–2d century C.E.) lists twenty-one hells, among which is the term *naraka,* which may denote hells in general or a particular hell.[8] There is not much in the way of description, perhaps because the details were considered common knowledge. What there is shares elements of the *Mahābhārata*'s description: "[The torture of] being tossed about in dreadful hells, Tāmisra and the rest, [that of] the Forest with sword-leaved trees and the like, and [that of] being bound and mangled (75); And various torments, the [pain of] being devoured by ravens and owls, the heat of scorching sand, and the [torture of] being boiled in jars, which is hard to bear (76)."[9]

Descriptions of hell are also found in the *Sūyagaḍa-sutta* (Distinction between good teachings and bad teachings, ca. 3d century B.C.E.) and the *Uttarajjhayaṇa-sutta* (Later responses, 1st or 2d century B.C.E.) of the Jainas, and these are also remarkably similar to those in Brahmanic sources. The following excerpts are from the *Sūyagaḍa-sutta,* "Description of the hells."

> Those cruel sinners who, from a desire of [worldly] life, commit bad deeds, will sink into the dreadful hell which is full of dense darkness and great suffering (3).
>
> . . . .
>
> Going to a place like a burning heap of coals on fire, and

> being burnt they cry horribly; they remain there long, shrieking aloud (7).
>
> Have you heard of the horrible [river] Vaitaraṇī, whose cutting waves are like sharp razors? They cross the horrible Vaitaraṇī, being urged on by arrows, and wounded with spears (8).
>
> . . . .
>
> And they come to the great impassable hell, full of agony, called Asūrya, where there is great darkness, where fires, placed above, below, and all around, are blazing (11).
>
> . . . .
>
> The prisoners in hell come to the dreadful place called Santakśaṇa, where the cruel punishers tie their hands and feet, and with axes in their hands cut them like wooden planks (14).
>
> And they turn the writhing victims round, and stew them, like living fishes, in an iron cauldron filled with their own blood, their limbs covered with ordure, their heads smashed (15).[10]

Similar themes continue in the second part of the section: sinners are mutilated, forced to walk over burning ground, crushed by rocks, scalded in cauldrons, skinned and devoured by iron-beaked birds, transfixed by pikes, burned in fires, beaten with clubs, devoured by jackals, and forced to descend into a river of molten iron.[11] A further description is found in the Jaina *Uttarajjhayaṇa-sutta* (Later readings), "The Son of Mṛgā."

> In the desert which is like a forest on fire, on the Vajravālukā and the Kadambavālukā rivers, I have been roasted an infinite number of times.
>
> Being suspended upside down over a boiler, shrieking, with no relation to help me, I was cut to pieces with various saws, an infinite number of times.
>
> I have suffered agonies when I was fastened with fetters on the huge Sālmalī tree, bristling with very sharp thorns, and then pushed up and down.

> An infinite number of times have I been crushed like sugarcane in presses, shrieking horribly, to atone for my sins, great sinner that I was.
>
> By black and spotted wild dogs I have, ever so many times, been thrown down, torn to pieces, and lacerated, screaming and writhing.
>
> When I was born in hell for my sins, I was cut, pierced, and hacked to pieces with swords and daggers, darts and javelins.
>
> I have been forcibly yoked to a car of red-hot iron full of fuel, I have been driven on with a goad and thongs, and have been knocked down like an antelope.
>
> On piles, in a blazing fire, I have forcibly been burnt and roasted like a buffalo, in atonement for my sins.
>
> An infinite number of times have I violently been lacerated by birds whose bills were of iron and shaped like tongs, by devilish vultures.
>
> Suffering from thirst I ran towards the river Vaitaraṇī to drink its water, but in it I was killed [as it were] by blades of razors.
>
> When suffering from the heat, I went into the forest in which the trees have a foliage of daggers; I have, ever so many times, been cut to pieces by the dropping dagger leaves.
>
> An infinite number of times have I suffered hopelessly from mallets and knives, forks and maces, which broke my limbs.
>
> Ever so many times have I been slit, cut, mangled, and skinned with keen-edged razors, knives, and shears (50–62).[12]

It is clear from the number of identical elements in the Brahmanic and Jaina texts that the two religions gained their knowledge from the same source. The Buddhist *Group of Discourses* also shows a relationship with them in verses 667–75. However, as we have already seen, the *Verses on the Law* does not contain the description of hell that became famous in later times. Each of these works was composed over such a long period of time that their dates are not very helpful in an accurate comparison of the texts. It is also virtually impossible to judge the relative age of the various concepts of hell according to content or treatment. Ancient Indian culture was anonymous; people freely adopted the ideas of others and used them as their own. Perhaps, too, the ideas were an ancient common heritage. In any case, it is impossible now to decide which religion influenced others in the concept of hell.

The eight hot hells. We will now examine the hells according to the *Abhidharmakośa*'s description. It shows a continuity, though not a direct one, with the *Group of Discourses* description (for example, in the names of some of the hells), and the influence of the Brahmanic and Jaina texts can also be seen there.

The main group of hells is termed the "great hells" or, more commonly, the "eight hot hells." The hells are located one below the other under Jambudvīpa, and are, from the topmost: Saṃjīva ("reviving"), Kālasūtra ("black string"), Saṃghāta ("dashing together"), Raurava ("weeping"), Mahāraurava ("great weeping"), Tāpana ("heating"), Pratāpana ("greatly heating"), and Avīci ("no release").

The bottom-most hell, Avīci, is the largest, a cube with each side 20,000 *yojanas* long. Its upper surface is 20,000 *yojanas* under the earth's surface, and its bottom surface is 40,000 *yojanas* under the earth's surface. In the 20,000 *yojanas* above the Avīci hell are found the remaining seven hells, but the *Abhidharmakośa* does not go into detail about their placement.

The *Great Commentary* (ca. 100–ca. 150 C.E.) gives three explanations concerning the positions of the eight hot hells. The first supplements the deficiencies in the *Abhidharmakośa.* The 20,000-*yojana* layer above the Avīci hell is occupied by the other seven hot hells, taking up the lower 19,000 *yojanas,* and the remainder is taken up by layers of white clay (the lower 500 *yojanas*) and mud (the upper 500 *yojanas*). In plane dimension, each of the seven hells is a square with sides of 10,000 *yojanas.* There is no mention of their depth. This is probably because it is not possible to divide 19,000 evenly by seven. The second explanation gives the Avīci hell as being 20,000 *yojanas* deeper than in the first explanation, making a space of 40,000 *yojanas* available. This space accommodates seven hot hells, cubes with sides of 5,000 *yojanas,* and four earth layers (from bottom to top: blue, yellow, red, white) each 1,000 *yojanas* deep, a white clay layer of 500 *yojanas,* and a mud layer, also 500 *yojanas.* Here the figures add up to exactly 40,000. The third explanation has the hells aligned horizontally, not vertically. The seven hot hells are grouped around the Avīci hell in the center, like small villages encircling a large castle.

Many doubts will inevitably be raised about the position of the hells. For example, since Jambudvīpa is given as being just 6,003.5 *yojanas* in circumference, how then can a number of larger hells exist beneath it? The Buddhist scholar-priests were not at a loss for an answer. They asserted that Jambudvīpa was pyramidal in shape, its surface pointed and its base wide, like a heap of grain spilled on the ground (see figures 7 and 15).

The kind of punishment given in each of these hells is apparent in their names. Some documents, though, do not clearly distinguish their characteristics, and the punishments seem similar in all of them. The *Abhidharmakośa*'s descriptions of the eight hells are less detailed than the other portrayals we have been discussing, so what follows is only a rough sketch.

The uppermost hell is Saṃjīva ("reviving"). Here evildoers are killed with blades, revived when a wind blows on their scattered remains, and forced to suffer the same torture again. People do not die just once here, but time and time again. This contrasts somewhat with the lowermost Avīci hell, where there is no respite at all from torture.[13] Beneath Saṃjīva is Kālasūtra ("black string"). Here evildoers are placed on boards, and lines are drawn on their bodies with black-inked thread, like the string that carpenters use to draw straight lines. The bodies are then cut along the lines. Next is Saṃghāta ("dashing together"). The element *saṃ* means "together," and *ghāta* means "slaughter." Here all sorts of sufferings are inflicted. Below it is Raurava

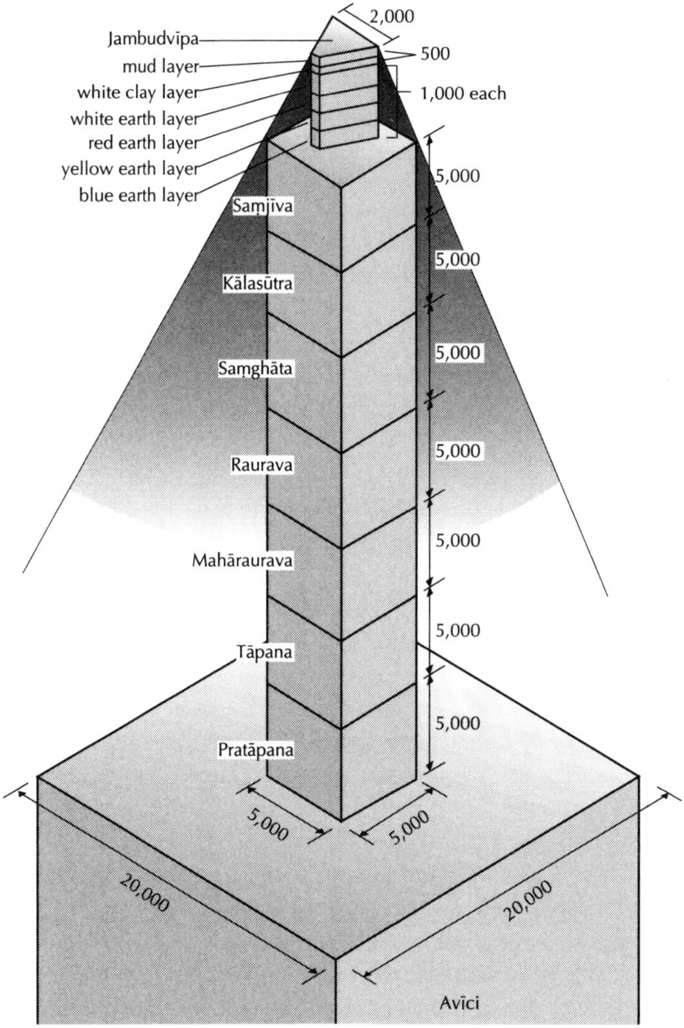

Fig. 15. Placement of the Eight Hot Hells according to the Second Interpretation in the *Great Commentary*

Note that Jambudvīpa is pyramidal in shape. Dimensions are given in *yojanas*.

("weeping"), where evildoers weep and cry because of the extent of their agony. The next hell, Mahāraurava ("great weeping"), inflicts even greater pain, so there is greater weeping. Tāpana ("heating") is a hell where evildoers suffer the torment of flames. The flames of Pratāpana ("greatly heating") cause even greater agony.

Various sūtras also depicted the hells, adding elements that stretch the imagination. One such sūtra is the *Sūtra of Stability in Contemplation of the True Dharma* (Saddharma-smṛty-upasthāna-sūtra, 538–43 C.E.). Its picture of the hells was used by the Japanese priest Genshin (942–1017) in his *Essentials of Salvation* (Ōjō yōshū). Let us look at the description of Saṃghāta in his work, in particular the section detailing the retribution for adultery.

> Further, the demons of hell seize those who have fallen into hell and put them into a forest, whose trees have leaves that are sword blades. As [the evildoers] look up to the treetops, they see beautiful, well-dressed women, whose faces have regular features. Seeing them, [the evildoers] immediately start climbing the trees, but when they do, the leaves pierce their flesh like swords and cut their sinews. When at last they reach the tops of the trees, their bodies all lacerated, they find that the women [suddenly] are below the trees, looking up at them with eyes full of passion and coquetry and saying, "For love of you I have come to this place. Why do you not come to where I am and embrace me?" Seeing [them] the evildoers, burning with passion, begin to climb down again. The blade-like leaves turn upward and lacerate their bodies as before. When they finally reach the bottom, the women again are at the tops of the trees. Seeing [this], the evildoers begin to climb the tree again. This continues for 10 trillion years. The cause of being thus deceived by their own minds and their continuous round of suffering and burning in this hell is their evil desire. . . .
>
> Connected with this hell are sixteen separate hells. Among

these is a hell called the Evil-Seeing Place. Those who have taken hold of the children of others and done evil things to them, causing them to weep and cry, fall into this hell and receive its agonies. They see their own children fallen into hell, tortured by the demons of hell, who thrust iron rods or iron gimlets into their genitals or drive iron hooks into their genitals. Seeing their children suffering so, the evildoers are filled with such love and pity that they cannot endure the sight. This suffering of seeing their children, however, is not one-sixteenth as great as the pain of being burned by fire. When the evildoers have been tortured thus in their minds, they are tortured physically. They are stood on their heads, and their vital organs and intestines are burned with molten copper that is poured [into the body] through the anus and, after burning the organs, comes out again from the mouth. These mental and physical sufferings continue unabated for immeasurable hundreds of thousands of years.

There is another special hell called "Much Suffering," into which fall those who have committed the evil of sodomy. Their torture is seeing those men [with whom they have had relations] in the past, so that their bodies burn with desire. When they approach and embrace the man, all the parts of their bodies fall away and are scattered.[14]

In the *Abhidharmakośa,* each of the eight hot hells has an entrance in each of its four sides, each entrance leading into four kinds of sub-hell (*utsada*), making a total of 128 sub-hells (see figure 16). The four kinds are Kukūla ("heated by burning chaff"), Kuṇapa ("corpses and dung"), Kṣuramārga ("razor road"), and Nadī Vaitaraṇī ("burning river").

In the first sub-hell, evildoers are forced to walk over hot ash. In the second they wallow in a quagmire of corpses and excrement, and maggots infest their skin, chewing the bone to the marrow. The third is of three kinds: (a) the razor road, where evildoers have to walk along a road of upward-facing sword blades; (b) the razor forest, where leaves like blades fall when

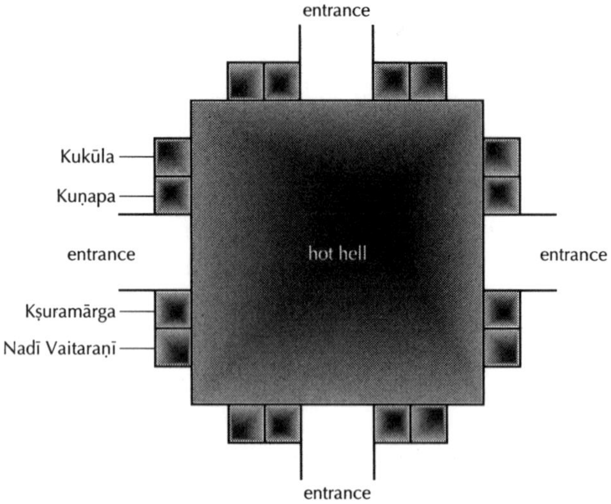

Fig. 16. A Hot Hell and Its Four Kinds of Sub-Hell, according to the *Abhidharmakośa*

the wind blows, nearly severing the evildoers' arms and legs, which are then pulled off and eaten by dogs with black spots; and (c) the forest of blades, where evildoers are forced at swordpoint to climb trees whose trunks are embedded with blades, so that if they try to climb up or down they are impaled, but if they stop hordes of ravens peck out and eat their eyes. The fourth is a hell in the form of a long, narrow moat or river of boiling water; evildoers are thrown in, tossed up to the surface, and drawn under again by the currents, like grains of rice. If they try to pull themselves out by putting their hands on the bank, guards sweep off their hands with swords and spears.

The eight cold hells. There are, in addition, eight cold hells, located below Jambudvīpa adjacent to the hot hells. Their names are Arbuda, Nirarbuda, Aṭaṭa, Hahava, Huhuva, Utpala, Padma, and Mahāpadma. Note the similarity of some of them to the names of the ten hells in the "Kokāliya" of the *Group of Discourses.*

As their designation suggests, these are the hells that torture evildoers through extreme cold. *Arbuda* means "abscess" or "swelling." The skin of those who fall into this hell breaks out in eruptions like frostbite, because of the intense cold. (Even today the Japanese call pockmarks *abata,* a word that derives from this Indic expression.) In Nirarbuda, the cold is even more intense, and the eruptions on the skin crack open. The names of the next three hells are onomatopoeic, describing the cries of the sufferers. The remaining three are names of lotuses. The *Abhidharmakośa* does not explain the connection between the lotus and the characteristics of the hells; earlier sources, however, such as the Chinese translation of the nineteenth sūtra in the *Long Discourses* and a footnote to the *Commentary on the Great Perfection of Wisdom Sūtra,* say that the name of each lotus indicates the color of the hell and its walls. Utpala ("blue lotus") refers to a blue-colored hell; Padma ("red lotus") to a red-colored hell; and Mahāpadma ("deep red lotus") to a crimson hell.

It is hard to understand how this description could cause terror, though perhaps the ancient Indians had some kind of psychological fear of these colors. The seventh-century commentary on the *Abhidharmakośa* by the Chinese priest P'u-kuang, *Chü-she-lun kuang-chi* (Memoir Illuminating the *Abhidharmakośa*), includes a more satisfying explanation. "The hell called Utpala is so named because the skin of an evildoer splits open because of the dreadful cold, and the body resembles a blue lotus. The hell called Padma is so named because here the skin splits and resembles a red lotus. The hell called Mahāpadma is so named because here the skin splits and resembles the great crimson lotus."[15] It is hard to say whether the image of bodies that are like blue, red, and crimson lotus flowers vying to bloom on the surface of a dark pond is horrifying or beautiful.

We have come to the end of the description of the hells, which total 144. The *Abhidharmakośa* also records the existence of "minor" hells, which are scattered from place to place. Unlike the hells we have seen so far, they are created from the karma of a small number of people. Though I will not take this topic any further, it strikes me that isolated hells like these where just one person is tortured are a terrifying concept.

REALMS OF ANIMALS, HUNGRY SPIRITS, AND *ASURAS*

The *Abhidharmakośa* describes animals, beings that move horizontally: "Animals may live in water, on the earth, or in the sky. They originated in the ocean and later moved from there to the land and sky."[16] This concept, of course, agrees with the modern theory of evolution.

Hungry spirits are the dead; the Sanskrit term *preta* means "the departed." The idea of hunger was added later to express the miserable condition in which the dead spirits were thought to exist. The original abode of these spirits lies 500 *yojanas* beneath Jambudvīpa. Among the dead spirits, some are virtuous and some are not. The former pass a pleasant life in groves and trees or escape this nether world to sport in heavenly palaces. The latter live in holes filled with urine and feces, and suffer from continuous hunger. The typical depiction of a hungry spirit without virtue is a being with a distended stomach and a long, thin neck like a needle who, though starving, cannot ingest anything through the throat (see photo 2). Some are shown managing to catch moths by attracting them to flames from their mouths, and others appear eating excrement, snivel, pus, and scum. In Japan a colloquial term for children is *gaki* ("hungry spirit") because of the large amount of food they eat. Yama is the king of the realm of hungry spirits; more will be said of him later.

Asuras dwell in the sea surrounding Mount Sumeru, and are considered inferior to human beings but superior to animals. They surpass human beings and match the *devas* in strength. Most are terrifying creatures, for they use their power for evil purposes. They are well known in Hinduism as being in constant battle with the *devas*, headed by Indra. In the famous drama

Śakuntalā, King Duḥśyanta chastised the *asuras* at the request of the *devas,* who were continually subjected to the *asuras'* violence.

In the most ancient sacred Hindu text, the *Ṛg Veda* (12th–8th century B.C.E.), however, *asura* had no such negative connotation. The word shares a common etymology with the *ahura* ("lord") of Zoroastrianism and signifies a god possessing mystical powers. *Asu* is interpreted as "breath"; *asura* therefore denotes a spiritual existence and is used as an epithet of Indra and Varuṇa. In India, though, *asura* eventually came to signify a demonic god. With the establishment of *asuras* as dark powers, interpretations of the etymology changed. *A* was interpreted as a negative prefix, and *sura* as "god" (*deva*), "drinking," or "delight and pleasure." All of these are possible meanings, but the most accurate is probably *asura* meaning "not-*deva,*" a being that is godlike but not a god.

The most famous *asura* is Rāhula Asura. According to the Chinese translation of the *Long Discourses,* this *asura* rules a great city 80,000 *yojanas* in length and breadth on the bed of the great ocean north of Mount Sumeru. The size, therefore, equals that of the ocean itself. Within the city are palaces, halls, and parks. Rāhula was not happy that the thirty-three gods, the sun, and the moon passed to and fro above his territory, so he fought with Indra and threatened to make earrings of the sun and moon. According to other sūtras, Rāhula sometimes leaves his dwelling beneath the sea and ascends Mount Sumeru to see the heavenly maidens. Unable to see them for the brightness of the sun, he covers the sun with his right hand. This creates a solar eclipse. When he covers the moon, a lunar eclipse occurs.

HEAVENS

It is a common pattern in Asian religions that hells below complement heavens above. In Buddhism, just as there are many hells, there are countless numbers of *devas,* and a multitude of heavens, summarized in figure 17.[17]

The Realm of the Four Great Kings (*Cātur-mahārāja-kāyikāḥ*). The part of Mount Sumeru that appears above the sea is a cube, each side 80,000 *yojanas* long. The Four Great Kings and their subordinates live in four separate tiers on the lower half of the cube (see figure 18). Ten thousand *yojanas* above the sea, a kind of terrace juts out 16,000 *yojanas* on all four sides, and another, 10,000 *yojanas* above the first, juts out 8,000 *yojanas*. Ten thousand *yojanas* above this there is yet another, which juts out 4,000 *yojanas*, and then a fourth, 10,000 *yojanas* higher, which juts out 2,000 *yojanas*. The tapered effect can no doubt be attributed to what we would call today the right to sunshine.

On the uppermost terrace live the Four Great Kings (also called the Four Heavenly Kings) and their servants. The kings are Dhṛtarāṣṭra, guardian of the east (in Japanese *Jikoku-ten*, "protector of the country"); Virūḍhaka, guardian of the south (in Japanese *Zōchō-ten*, "one who gains power"); Virūpākṣa, guardian of the west (in Japanese *Kōmoku-ten*, "wide eyes"); and Vaiśravaṇa, guardian of the north (in Japanese *Tamon-ten*, *Bishamon-ten*, "much hearing"). The roles of these kings are not explained well in the texts. Their subordinates live on the lower three tiers, in the seven mountain ranges, and on the sun and moon (which revolve at a height halfway up the mountain).

The heaven of the thirty-three gods. On the summit of Mount Sumeru is the heaven of the thirty-three gods (*trayas-triṃśāḥ*), whose roles are also somewhat mysterious, except for Indra. The summit is an area 80,000 *yojanas* square, with a peak in each corner 500 *yojanas* tall, where the Vajra-pāṇi live, demigods called *yakṣas*. In the middle of that heaven is a city called Lovely View (Sudarśana), 2,500 *yojanas* square and 1.5 *yojanas* high. Its buildings are made of gold, and its ground is of a cotton-like substance (a cloud, perhaps) called *tūlapicu*. In the center of the city is a palace, 250 *yojanas* square, called the Palace of Victory (Vaijayanta). Adorned with various kinds of jewels, it is peerless. Here dwells the greatest of the thirty-three gods, Indra (Śakro devānām indraḥ). The Buddhist Indra, of course, derives from the Brahmanic deity of that name. (See figure 19 for the dwellings of the other thirty-two gods.) There are four parks in the four directions of the city, called Caitra-ratha, Pāruṣya, Miśra, and Nandana. These names seem to derive either from the names of their makers or from the names of the trees planted in them. For example, in the *Mahābhārata,* Caitra-ratha is the garden of the god Kubera, made by the *gandharva* Citra-ratha, one of Indra's demigod musicians. Pāruṣya might be a garden containing trees like aloe (*pāruṣya*). In the same source, Nandana appears as the name of Indra's garden. On the four sides of each of these gardens are pleasure areas, each twenty *yojanas* distant from its garden. Outside the city on the northeast corner is a tree called a *pārijāta,* and on the southwest corner, a hall called Sudharman. The roots of the *pārijāta* tree stretch fifty *yojanas* into the earth (which is actually sand made up of the four jewels), and its trunk and leaves extend 100 *yojanas* into the sky. The scent of its flowers and leaves is carried one hundred *yojanas* in a favorable wind and fifty in an adverse wind.

The six abodes of the gods of the realm of desire. The abodes of the Four Great Kings and their subordinates and the abode of the thirty-three gods are of the earthly realm, whereas the other four abodes of the gods of the realm of desire belong to the aerial sphere. The inhabitants of all six of these abodes belong to the realm of desire (*kāma-dhātu*), differing little from human beings in their actions, although their power is much greater. Ethically, theirs remains an imperfect existence, for desires still hold them captive. Still, some have proceeded farther along the way of religious training than others. Although they all burn with the flames of the passions, the higher the heaven in which they dwell, the more sublimated is their method of quenching their passion. For example, the gods of the earthly realm (the Four Great Kings and the thirty-three gods) cannot quench their desires without sexual contact, but their passion, unlike men's,

				DISTANCE FROM THE WATER SURFACE OF THE GOLDEN EARTH LAYER
Heavenly deities	Realm of form	Fourth Dhyāna	Akaniṣṭha	(*yojanas*) 167,772,160,000
			Sudarśana	83,886,080,000
			Sudṛśa	41,943,040,000
			Atapa	20,971,520,000
			Abṛha	10,485,760,000
			Bṛhatphala	5,242,880,000
			Puṇyaprasava	2,621,440,000
			Anabhraka	1,310,720,000
		Third Dhyāna	Śubhakṛtsna	(*yojanas*) 655,360,000
			Apramāṇaśubha	327,680,000
			Parīttaśubha	163,840,000
		Second Dhyāna	Ābhāsvara	(*yojanas*) 81,920,000
			Apramāṇābha	40,960,000
			Parīttābha	20,480,000
		First Dhyāna	Mahābrahmā	(*yojanas*) 10,240,000
			Brahma-purohita	5,120,000
			Brahma-kāyika	2,560,000
	Realm of desire	Six Heavens of the realm of desire	Para-nirmita-vaśavartin heaven	(*yojanas*) 1,280,000
			Nirmāṇa-rati heaven	640,000
			Tuṣita heaven	320,000
			Yama heaven	160,000
Earth-dwelling deities			Heaven of the thirty-three gods	(*yojanas*) 80,000
			Heaven of the Four Great Kings and their subordinates	40,000
Above the ground			Uttarakuru	(*yojanas*) 0
			Aparagodānīya	0
			Pūrvavideha	0
			Jambudvīpa	0
			Realm of the animals	(*yojanas*) 0
Below the earth			Realm of the spirits of the dead	500
			Saṃjīva	(*yojanas*) 1,000
			Kālasūtra	unclear
			Saṃghāta	unclear
			Raurava	unclear
			Mahāraurava	unclear
			Tāpana	unclear
			Pratāpana	unclear
			Avīci	20,000

Fig. 17. Relationship of the Realms of Desire and Form
One *krośa* is a bit less than a kilometer. One *hasta* is the length of a forearm. One *kalpa* is an incalculably long period of time. One great *kalpa* equals eighty *kalpas*.

AREA	HUMAN HEIGHT	HUMAN LIFE SPAN
one great-thousand-world	(*yojanas*) 16,000.0	(one great *kalpa*) 16,000.0
one great-thousand-world	8,000.0	8,000.0
one great-thousand-world	4,000.0	4,000.0
one great-thousand-world	2,000.0	2,000.0
one great-thousand-world	1,000.0	1,000.0
one great-thousand-world	500.0	500.0
one great-thousand-world	250.0	250.0
one great-thousand-world	125.0	125.0
one medium-thousand-world	(*yojanas*) 64.0	(one great *kalpa*) 64.0
one medium-thousand-world	32.0	32.0
one medium-thousand-world	16.0	16.0
one small-thousand-world	(*yojanas*) 8.0	(one great *kalpa*) 8.0
one small-thousand-world	4.0	4.0
one small-thousand-world	2.0	2.0
area as broad as the four landmasses	(*yojanas*) 1.5	(half a great *kalpa*) 1.5
area as broad as the four landmasses	1.0	1.0
area as broad as the four landmasses	0.5	0.5
(*yojanas*) $80{,}000^2$	(*krośas*) 1.50	(years) 16,000 x 1,600 x 30 x 12
$80{,}000^2$	1.25	8,000 x 800 x 30 x 12
$80{,}000^2$	1.00	4,000 x 400 x 30 x 12
$80{,}000^2$	0.75	2,000 x 200 x 30 x 12
(*yojanas*) $80{,}000^2$	(*krośas*) 0.50	(years) 1,000 x 100 x 30 x 12
various	0.25	500 x 50 x 30 x 12
(*yojanas*) $2{,}000^2$	(*hastas*) 32	(years) 1,000
$1{,}250^2\pi$	16	500
about 2,000,000	8	250
about 2,000,000	4	infinite–10
unclear	unclear	at most, one *kalpa*
unclear	unclear	500 x 30
(*yojanas*) unclear	unclear	(years) 500 x 30 x 12 x (500 x 50 x 30 x 12)
unclear	unclear	1,000 x 30 x 12 x (1,000 x 100 x 30 x 12)
unclear	unclear	2,000 x 30 x 12 x (2,000 x 200 x 30 x 12)
unclear	unclear	4,000 x 30 x 12 x (4,000 x 400 x 30 x 12)
unclear	unclear	8,000 x 30 x 12 x (8,000 x 800 x 30 x 12)
unclear	unclear	16,000 x 30 x 12 x (16,000 x 1,600 x 30 x 12)
unclear	unclear	half a *kalpa*
$20{,}000^2$	unclear	one *kalpa*

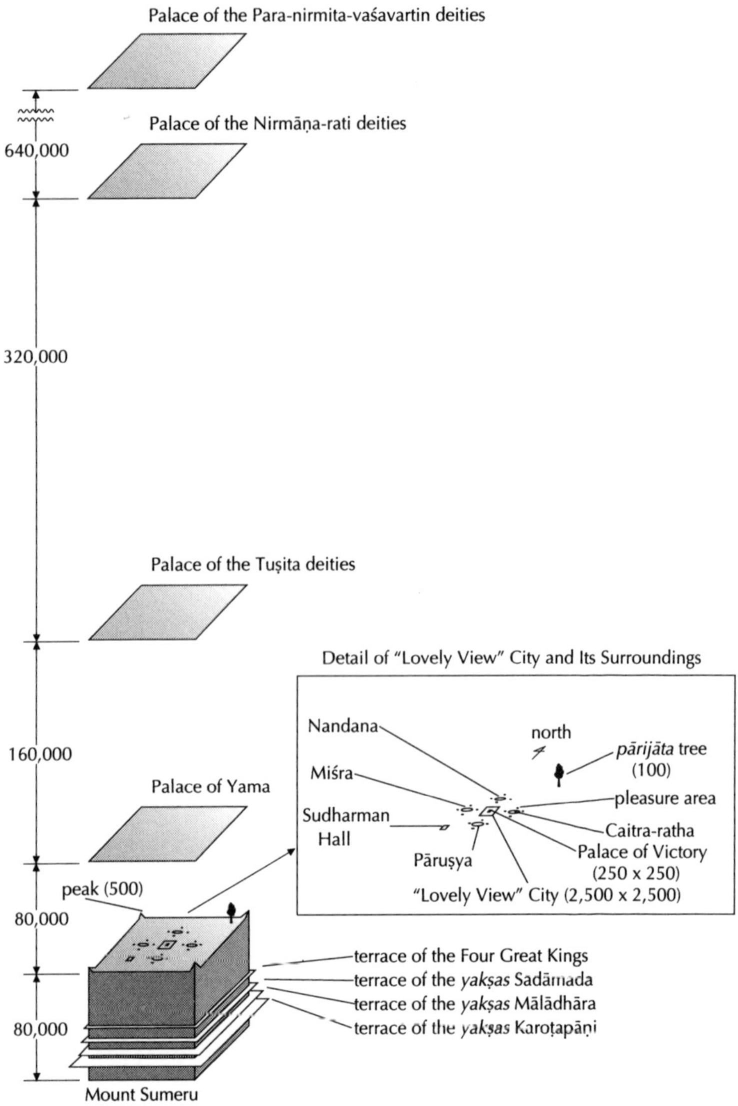

Fig. 18. Dwellings of the Thirty-Three Gods
Dimensions are given in *yojanas*.

Fig. 19. Detailed Plan of the Dwellings of the Thirty-Three Gods
This figure is the "Drawing of the Tuṣita Heaven" that appears in the thirty-first fascicle of the *Fo-tsu t'ung-chi* (Record of the lineage of the Buddha and patriarchs), compiled in 1258–69 by Chih-p'an. This is a detail of the square land that appears in the inset in figure 18. The drawing should, in fact, be square, not round. The area shown in black in the center of the square land in figure 18, the Palace of Victory belonging to Indra, occupies the center of this drawing as well. The other thirty-two gods dwell in palaces outside its walls in the city called Lovely View. Between the palace of Indra and those of the other gods are the markets for foodstuffs, clothing, grains, and entertainment.

disperses with the ejection not of semen but of wind. In this sense they are considered higher than human beings. In the case of the inhabitants of the four aerial realms, gods in the Yama heaven are able to fulfill their passion through a simple embrace, those in the Tuṣita heaven through clasping the hands, those in the Nirmāṇa-rati heaven through a smiling glance, and those in the Para-nirmita-vaśavartin heaven through a glance alone.

Children are conceived through wind rather than semen. The process of birth is also different from that of human beings. The *Abhidharmakośa* says, "There are both male and female deities; *deva* boys and *deva* girls are born upon their knees."[18] The higher the heaven, the more mature children are at birth. Children of the Four Great Kings and their attendants appear to be five years old at birth; those of the thirty-three gods, six; those of the inhabitants of the Yama heaven, seven; those of the Tuṣita heaven, eight; those of the Nirmāṇa-rati heaven, nine; and those of the Para-nirmita-vaśavartin heaven, ten. This picture of deities with wives and children leading a life of pleasure is somewhat different from our usual picture of a god.

Eighty thousand *yojanas* above the summit of Mount Sumeru is the heavenly palace (*vimāna*) of Yama and his attendants, 80,000 *yojanas* square, the same size as the summit of Sumeru. There is no indication of how deeply it extends. Yama is known in Japan as Emma, lord of the dead. (We shall see in chapter 8 why he lives here, rather than in hell.) One hundred sixty thousand *yojanas* above Yama's palace is the palace of the Tuṣita deities (from *tuṣita,* "satisfied"); the Tuṣita may be deities who know satisfaction. A further 320,000 *yojanas* above this is the abode of the Nirmāṇa-rati, the deities who create their own enjoyment, and then 640,000 *yojanas* higher the palace of the Para-nirmita-vaśavartins (meaning "who can change the pleasure created by others into [his own pleasure]"). These gods may desire not so much their own pleasure as to create pleasure themselves, and they are advanced in relinquishing desire. In size all these abodes are the same as the palace of Yama.

The Realm of the *Dhyāna* Practitioner

So far we have seen a universe with inhabitants living on the earth, in hells, in the realm of hungry spirits, and in heavens. It shares many elements with the cosmologies of other religions. Buddhism, though, is perhaps unique in positing an additional realm of *dhyāna* practitioners above the realm of gods. This consists of the "realm of form" (*rūpa-dhātu*) and the "realm of formlessness" (*ārūpya-dhātu*).

Form (*rūpa*) is that which has shape and is characterized by constant change and destruction. *Rūpa-dhātu,* therefore, is where those having form dwell. Of course the possession of form is a condition shared also by those who occupy the realm of desire (*kāma-dhātu*). Nevertheless when we speak of the realm of form we do not include the realm of desire, for those who dwell there have gained release from all desires, so that only their physical bodies remain. This is the realm of those who practice *dhyāna* ("meditation"), which includes the two practices of "quieting the mind" and "observing the nature of things." Buddhist priests, and indeed we ourselves, may climb to a realm higher than that inhabited by the gods by pursuing the practice of meditation to its limits.

The realm of form is divided broadly into four areas, the First through Fourth Dhyānas (in ascending order). The First Dhyāna consists of three Brahmā realms: Brahma-kāyika, where the subordinates of Brahmā dwell; Brahma-purohita, where the attendants, ministers, and officials of Brahmā dwell; and Mahābrahmā, "great Brahmā." The realm of Brahma-kāyika is 1,280,000 *yojanas* above the highest heaven of the realm of desire, Para-nirmita-vaśavartin. Its extent is "as broad as the four landmasses," Pūrvavideha, Jambudvīpa, Aparagodānīya, and Uttarakuru. This is an extremely vague expression, but one possibility is that it means the area of a circle whose circumference is described around the four points that are the landmasses (see figure 20). If we consider that the four landmasses are located in the center of the salt sea, the area would thus be a circle with a radius of 420,086.5 *yojanas*. The inhabitants of this heaven have bodies half a *yojana* tall. The heaven of Brahma-purohita is 2,560,000 *yojanas* above Brahmakāyika and is the same size as the latter. Its inhabitants are one *yojana* tall. If the populations of the two were the same, those living in Brahma-purohita might be rather cramped. Still, because they are officials, they may be fewer in number. Mahābrahmā is 5,120,000 *yojanas* above Brahma-purohita and is the same size. Its inhabitants are 1.5 *yojanas* tall.

Though we are now in the realm of form, the First Dhyāna is still concerned with the world of myth. Brahmā was originally a Brahmanic god, the highest of the pantheon. He appears in the First Dhyāna more as a symbol of separation from desires and of purity than as a god per se. The Mahābrahmā heaven reminds us of the possibility of gaining release from the realm of desire through meditation, and is the realm where those whose

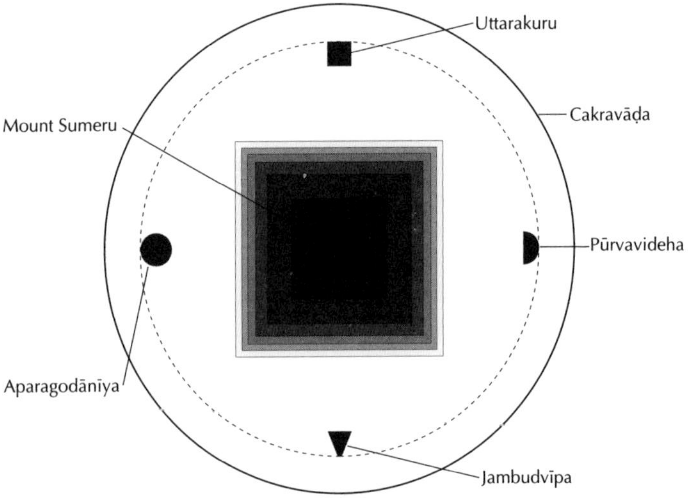

Fig. 20. Extent of the First Dhyāna Heavens
The broken line shows one possible meaning of "an area as broad as the four landmasses."

virtue is equal to that of Brahmā himself gather. The various mind functions of the deities of the First Dhyāna have not yet stopped working, but these deities take joy in the fact that they have nothing to do with desires or with anything evil.

The Second Dhyāna also has three heavens; in ascending order, these are Parīttābha ("limited radiance"), Apramāṇābha ("boundless radiance"), and Ābhāsvara ("ultimate radiant purity"). All of them are replete with virtue, symbolized by various kinds of light. Parīttābha is 10,240,000 *yojanas* above the Mahābrahmā heaven, Apramāṇābha is 20,480,000 *yojanas* above Parīttābha, and Ābhāsvara is 40,960,000 *yojanas* above Apramāṇābha. They are all the same size, one "small-thousand-world." (A "small single world" denotes a volume of space incorporating all of the realm of desire and the First Dhyāna of the realm of form. A "small-thousand-world" is a measure of one thousand such "small worlds.") Whether we can assign a position to this vast space is somewhat doubtful (see figure 21). In the realm of the Second Dhyāna there is no discursive thought or reasoning. All that remains is the delight born of intensely tranquil and concentrated meditation (*samādhi*).

Like the First and Second Dhyānas, the Third Dhyāna has three heavens, which are, in ascending order, Parīttaśubha ("limited purity"), Apramāṇaśubha ("unlimited purity"), and Śubhakṛtsna ("complete purity"). Parīttaśubha is 81,920,000 *yojanas* above the highest stratum of the Second Dhyāna, Ābhāsvara; Apramāṇaśubha is 163,840,000 *yojanas* above Parīttaśubha; and Śubhakṛtsna is a further 327,680,000 *yojanas* above Apramāṇaśubha. In size, each is a medium-thousand-world, that is, one thousand small-thousand-worlds. In the Third Dhyāna, all joy in meditation is eliminated and only a sublime delight remains, experienced when the meditator is one with truth. There is no greater tranquillity, and it may be the equivalent of what Greek philosophy terms *ataraxia*, imperturbability of mind and body, the goal of human life.

The first three Dhyāna realms are alike in that delight (*sukha*) remains. Therefore they are termed *sukha-upapatti*, "realms of

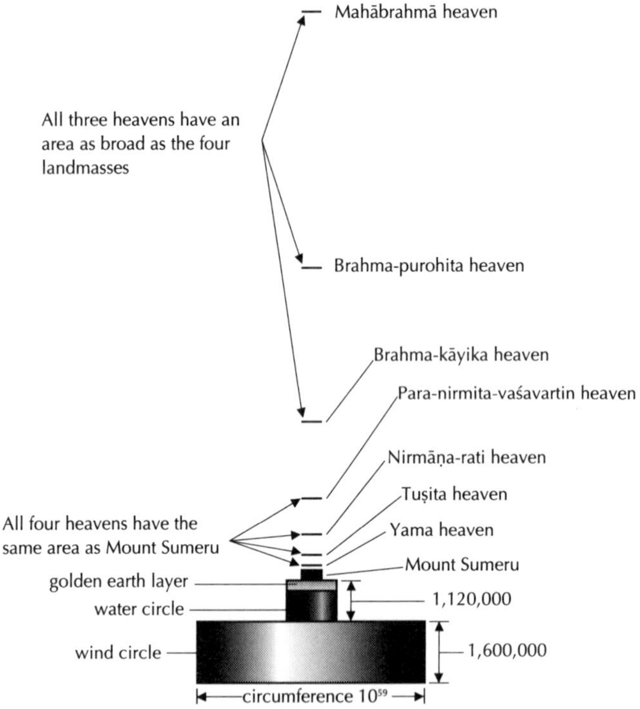

Fig. 21. Composition of a World
Dimensions are given in *yojanas.*

delight." The realm of form does not end here, however. Next is the Fourth Dhyāna, the stage where all suffering and all delight have been transcended. It is made up of eight heavens, which I list without going into the subtle differences among them, leaving that to more scholarly studies. They are: Anabhraka ("cloudless gods"), Puṇyaprasava ("gods produced by virtue"), Bṛhatphala ("gods of great fruit"), Abṛha ("undefiled gods"), Atapa ("gods of no heat"), Sudṛśa ("gods looking handsome"), Sudarśana (also "gods looking handsome"), and Akaniṣṭha ("gods of the extremity of the realm of form"). All of the gods, from those of Brahmā to those of Akaniṣṭha, belong to the realm of form and are therefore material, with physical bodies. In the realm of formlessness, however, no material form remains, only spirit. This realm is discussed in the "Enlightenment" section of chapter 3.

3. Transmigration, Karma, and Enlightenment

When asked why the wind circle upholding the Sumeru realm did not disperse, Indian scholars said that it was held together by the force of the *karma* ("action") of living beings. Indians believed that all action leaves behind results; good actions leave good results, and evil actions leave evil results. Therefore, action does not disappear as soon as it is completed. An unseen force remains, the consequence of both individual actions and the actions of all living beings taken together. Buddhism calls the entirety of action, including its results, *combined karma* or *common karma*. It is this combined karma that prevents the wind circle from dispersing.

The ideas of karma and transmigration are the foundation of Buddhist cosmology, whose purpose is to illuminate their nature and relationship to human existence. Unlike the modern scientific view of the cosmos, Buddhist cosmology is meaningless without the human element.

The Six Destinations of Rebirth

Transmigration (*saṃsāra*) means the repeated cycle of birth and death in this realm of delusion. Literally "flowing together," *saṃsāra* is an expression of living beings buffeted by waves and at the mercy of water, perhaps a powerful river whose current carries us from place to place. As we have seen, rebirth has five or six destinations. The *Abhidharmakośa* gives five—the inhabitants of hells, hungry spirits, animals, human beings, and *devas*. This is the Sarvāstivādin point of view; other schools gave six, the above five plus the *asuras*.[1] In Chinese and Japanese Buddhism, the version favoring six paths gained popularity, and the expression "transmigration among the six paths" is well known throughout East Asia. According to the *Commentary on the Great Perfection of Wisdom Sūtra*, the six paths are divided into three good and three bad, and further into superior, ordinary, and inferior (see figure 14).

It is obvious how the inhabitants of hells, hungry spirits, and animals could be considered bad destinations in the realm of delusion. *Asuras* and human beings on the other hand, though good destinations, are also inhabitants of the realm of delusion. The unclean nature of human existence is emphasized in a meditation called "contemplation of impurity," in which meditation subjects include human excreta and the internal organs. (Genshin has a good example of this in *Essentials of Salvation*.) Zen priests also call the human being a bag of dung.

The gods, too, are inhabitants of the realm of delusion. They may have received the most pleasant existence of the six paths, but they are still subject to the three poisons of greed, anger, and ignorance, so they may eventually fall into the realms of the hells or the hungry spirits. The *Sūtra of Cause and Effect in the Past and Present* (Kuo-ch'u-hsien-tsai-yin-kuo-ching, trans. into Chinese 5th century) says, "When fortune is exhausted, there comes suffering; on the six paths of transmigration, eventually suffering accumulates."[2] Because the inhabitants of the six paths of rebirth, including the devas, all dwell in the realm of desire, they are all subject to suffering.

The idea of rebirth is also reflected in biographies of the Buddha. The Buddha experiences a variety of previous births, during which he practices his religious discipline and appears as a perfected being. The *Jātakas*, tales of the Buddha's former lives, relate how he amasses great numbers of virtues. In some of them, he is shown as having been born previously as a monkey or a deer.

The Force of Karma

Of equal importance to the idea of transmigration is the concept of karma. *Karma* (also *karman*) means "action," and it consists of both action and its power of influence. "Action" does not refer just to bodily movements, but also includes the actions of speech and mind. An action's power of influence is not confined to this life but extends to future lives as well.

Karma affects the destiny of the entire natural realm, not only that of the individual. For example, when the universe is about to come into being, a subtle wind begins to stir, and what causes it to quicken is "the indirect force of the karma of the various living beings." The water circle that eventually develops is prevented from dispersing because "it is maintained by the force of the karma of all living beings." This force also creates the hells and the heavens. In Buddhism, this combined karmic force is called common karma.[3]

Karma functions automatically, without the need of some kind of godlike arbitrator. Meritorious acts give rise to good results, and evil causes adverse results. This is a law analogous to natural law. Each person receives upon him- or herself the retributions or rewards for his or her own acts. That is why Buddhist texts do not say "to be punished" or "to be thrown into hell," as though a god were the agent, but rather "to receive retribution" and "to fall into hell." Similarly, we will see in chapter 4 that those whose retribution in hell has not been completed will, at the end of this universe, be moved to a hell in another universe.

Ājīvika Ideas about Transmigration

Scholars of Indian intellectual history take continuing interest in the question of the origin of particular ideas, and transmigration is no exception. There is, though, no idea that is more lost in the mists of history than this one. I do not intend to discuss the question of its origin here, for it would be far too great a task. I wish, instead, to examine the idea of transmigration in the non-Buddhist philosophies that arose in India and Greece at much the same time as Buddhism. This will, perhaps, serve as a stepping stone to further study for interested readers.

The idea of transmigration hardly appears in the Hindu *Ṛg Veda* (12th–8th century B.C.E.), though by the time the new religious movements arose in the sixth to fifth centuries B.C.E., most of the important ones included a philosophy of transmigration, outstanding examples being Buddhism, Jainism, and the religion of the Ājīvikas. We also find the idea in Brahmanism in the new literature called the *Upaniṣads*. Here I would like to examine the idea as it appears among the Ājīvika sect.

According to the founder, Makkhali Gosāla,

> There are 1,406,600 kinds of living being. There are 500 karmas, 5 karmas, 3 karmas, 1 karma, and a half karma. There are 62 practices, 62 intermediate *kalpas,* 6 classes, 8 stages, 4,900 modes of living, 4,900 wandering mendicants, 4,900 Nāgā realms, 2,000 organs, 3,000 hells, 36 polluted realms, 7 thinking beings, 7 non-thinking beings, 7 insects, 7 heavenly beings, 7 human beings, 7 demons, 7 lakes, 7 mountains, 707 impregnable passes, 707 dreams. There are 8,400,000 great *kalpas* [extremely long periods of time]. During that time both the ignorant and the wise undergo rebirth, and being reborn, bring about the end of suffering. During that time no one can say, "Through practice of the precepts, or through practice of the purities, or through asceticism, or through chastity, I will bring to maturity that karma still immature. And I will gradually gain liberation from the karma already matured." The pleasure and suffering have already been meted out and will continue without increase or decrease during the course of the round of birth and death. It is like a ball of thread that must be unraveled to the end. Both the ignorant and the wise must undergo the round of birth and death until the end of suffering is reached.[4]

Living beings transmigrate among all types of existence. So far, Gosāla agrees with Buddhism. He differs, however, in saying that meritorious activities such as religious practice and asceticism are of no use in gaining liberation from the round of birth and death. According to Gosāla, human destiny is fixed. As a ball of thread unravels, birth and death will continue until the stipulated end, whatever religious exercises a person might undertake. It was natural that Buddhism, with its emphasis on the importance of religious training, would reject this idea as fatalism (*nyativāda*).

Greek Ideas about Transmigration

Among Greek ideas about transmigration, that of Orphism is particularly well known. In this theory, transmigration was said to occur as a result of sins committed. Followers of Orphism therefore had to maintain the precepts strictly and purify their lives, so that they could release their spirits from their bodies, at which point the spirits were believed to return to Dionysus. Pythagoras (ca. 580–ca. 500 B.C.E.) was a follower of the Orphic cult, and he founded a sect. A famous episode tells how, when he was out walking, he came across a man whipping a dog. He cried out, "Stop that! That dog you are beating is an old friend of mine! He has now been reborn as a dog, but I know his voice."[5]

Empedocles (ca. 490–430 B.C.E.), a theoretician of elements, wrote, "The father fishes up his beloved dead child, now reborn as a fish, and kills him. And the fool even gives thanks to the gods! But they [his servants] hesitate to sacrifice one who seeks compassion. The father does not hear the cries [of the sacrificial victim] and after having killed him, prepares an evil meal within his house. In the same way sons capture fathers, children capture mothers, and take their lives and eat that dear meat."[6]

According to the Greek historian Herodotus (ca. 484–ca. 425 B.C.E.), the idea of transmigration came to Greece from Egypt.

"The Egyptians say that Demeter [Isis] and Dionysus [Osiris] are the chief powers in the underworld; and they were also the first people to put forward the doctrine of the immortality of the soul, and to maintain that after death it enters another creature at the moment of that creature's birth. It then makes the round of all living things—animals, birds, and fish—until it finally passes once again, at birth, into the body of a man. The whole period of transmigration occupies three thousand years. This theory has been adopted by certain Greek writers, some earlier, some later, who have put it forward as their own. Their names are known to me, but I refrain from mentioning them."[7]

What we should note is that the Greeks believed that the soul transmigrated, while Buddhism denied the existence of the soul. In the Buddhist work *Milinda's Questions* (Milindapañha, compiled 1st century B.C.E.–1st century C.E.), the Greek King Menandros (Menander) questions the Buddhist Nāgasena about the seeming contradiction between the Buddhist ideas of rebirth and a non-self. The king asks how rebirth takes place without anything transmigrating, and Nāgasena replies as follows:

> "It is as if, sire, some person might light a lamp. Would it burn all night long?"
> "Yes, revered sir, it might burn all night long."
> "Is the flame of the first watch the same as the flame of the middle watch?"
> "No, revered sir."
> "Is the flame of the middle watch the same as the flame of the third watch?"
> "No, revered sir."
> "Is it then, sire, that the lamp in the first watch was one thing, the lamp in the middle watch another, and the lamp in the last watch still another?"
> "O no, revered sir, it was burning all through the night in dependence on itself."
> "Even so, sire, a continuity of dhammas ["beings, existences, persons"] runs on; one uprises, another ceases; it runs on as

though there were no before, no after; consequently neither the one [dhamma] nor another is reckoned as the last consciousness."[8]

This passage states the belief of Buddhists that there is no continuous and eternal "I." While the lamp burns, the flame changes from moment to moment, yet it is as if it were the same flame. The flame of the first watch is the "I" of the present, and the flame of the middle watch is the "I" of the future.

The fact that the idea of transmigration was current in both India and Greece at around the same time is surprising and puzzling. Is it possible that there was some borrowing between the two cultures? The Roman officer Arrian mentions the legend that Dionysus invaded India.[9] If we give some credence to this as evidence of contact between the two cultures, we can allow that there was some connection between Greek and Indian transmigration theories. The question of which culture affected the other remains. There is also the possibility that there may have been an indirect relationship through a third culture.

Enlightenment and the Realm of Formlessness

In previous chapters we have discussed the dwelling places among which living beings transmigrate according to karma. But where does the Buddha dwell? Mahāyāna Buddhism posits its own theories about this, which are discussed in part 2. In terms of the *Abhidharmakośa*, however, the Buddha probably occupies a position above the realm of formlessness, where old maps of Mount Sumeru show him. To be accurate, however, the realm of the Buddha is beyond space.

Where, then, is the realm of formlessness (*ārūpya-dhātu*)? In that realm, beings no longer have physical, material bodies. There is only spirit, and no form (*rūpa*) remains. We should not assume that the realm of formlessness is "above" the realm of form, for it transcends all geographical notions. Though we include it in cosmology, it is completely detached from spatial concepts. It is not, however, beyond the reach of time, and the inhabitants of its various levels follow allotted life spans of twenty thousand great *kalpas,* eighty thousand great *kalpas,* etc. (A *kalpa* is a period of time so long that it cannot be calculated in years.)

Before he became a buddha, Siddhārtha, on taking up the religious life, studied under the ascetic Ārāḍa Kālāma and attained the Four Dhyānas and the *samādhis* of the Four Formless Abodes, which were subsequently incorporated into Buddhism. These Four Abodes are termed Ākāśa-ānantya-āyatana ("abode of the infinity of space"), Vijñāna-ānantya-āyatana ("abode of the infinity of consciousness"), Ākiṃcanya-āyatana ("abode of nothingness"), and Naiva-saṃjñā-nāsaṃjñā-āyatana ("abode of neither thought nor non-thought").

Samādhi. We have seen that practitioners of *dhyāna* may attain any of the various Dhyāna heavens in the realm of form. The realm of formlessness, however, belongs to practitioners of *samādhi.* There is a subtle difference between the two. *Dhyāna* incorporates the practices of tranquillity ("quieting the mind") and discernment ("observing the nature of things"). *Samādhi* involves an intensification of the elements of tranquillity. In the broadest sense of the word, it means concentration of the mind on one point, and so includes *dhyāna. Samādhi* is an element of religious training that has been consistently emphasized in both pre-Mahāyāna and Mahāyāna Buddhism (especially in the Wisdom sūtras).

Each of the Four Formless Abodes is attained by means of a corresponding kind of *samādhi.* For example, when one has attained the Ākāśa-ānantya-āyatana *samādhi,* one dwells in the abode of the infinity of space. To enter this abode means that all thoughts of the realm of form are eliminated, and only infinite space remains. The *Commentary on the Great Perfection of Wisdom Sūtra* sets out in specific terms how this may be achieved: "Contemplate space within the body, and always contemplate the body as being void, like a cage, or like a receptacle for steam cooking. . . . Thus [you] are enabled to transcend form and eliminate the body. As the body becomes infinite space, so does other outer form. At that time [you] have succeeded in contemplating the emptiness of the infinity of space."[10]

The concept of the four *samādhis* is subtle, and I fear that I, not having ascended to such heights (170 billion *yojanas* above Jambudvīpa!), scarcely have the qualifications to discuss their differences. Nevertheless I will attempt a simple explanation. The goal of *samādhi* practitioners is the realm of the absolute, a realm where the self is at one with the universe, in which all relativity has vanished. From the practitioner's standpoint, it means liberation from the "small self"[11] to seek the state of freedom. I deal with the idea of the absolute later, but here I discuss the *samādhi* of the four stages from the viewpoint of freedom.

Even in the realm of form practitioners attain considerable freedom, though strictly in terms of the material world. In the realm of formlessness, the practitioner has freedom from the material, and strives to attain perfect spiritual freedom, realized only when the practitioner removes all thought objects. When thought objects exist, one remains in the grip of the *idea* of the final stage. In the first stage of the realm of formlessness, the mind has to enter the realm of infinite space (infinite voidness) in order to eliminate thought objects concerning the material. This is the *samādhi* of the abode of the infinity of space.

Upon reflection, though, the practitioner realizes that infinite space is itself an object (what the fifth-century B.C.E. Greek philosophers Leucippus and Democritus called "not-being being not inferior to being"). Therefore the mind must next do away with infinite space as a thought object and gain liberation from that condition. At that point, the practitioner enters a realm from which all thought objects have been eliminated, a realm in which only mind itself exists. This is Vijñāna-ānantya-āyatana (the abode of the infinity of consciousness).

Upon still further reflection, the practitioner comes to realize that the *thought* of "the elimination of all thought objects" does remain, and liberation must be gained from that. One must proceed to eliminate all thoughts of having done something, of having gained liberation from a lower stage and ascended to a higher one, or of having attained the fruit of practice, so that one may enter the realm of having nothing at all. This is Ākiṃcanya-āyatana (the abode of nothingness).

Again on further reflection, one realizes that even nothingness is an idea that one holds, and it is necessary to eliminate this, too. Then one enters Naiva-saṃjñā-nāsaṃjñā-āyatana (the abode of neither thought nor non-thought). "Non-thought" is "not thinking," which itself becomes the "thought of not-thinking." It must therefore be negated as well, which gives us "nor non-thought." This is considered the highest of the stages.[12] (By this logic, however, we must admit that it cannot be called the last stage at all, and we could continue the process infinitely.) A *buddha* (literally, "one who has attained enlightenment") ascends to the abode of neither thought nor non-thought, and then transcends the three realms and gains liberation from the cycle of transmigration.

A buddha's mission is to rescue living beings trapped in the worlds of transmigration. A buddha appears in the world as a result of his aspiration toward enlightenment in former existences and his accumulation of various kinds of practice in order to fulfill a vow. It is said that only one buddha appears in a single world system (or, some say, in a trichiliocosm, described in chapter 4). Śākyamuni, the buddha who appeared in India, was one such buddha.

To attain enlightenment is not an easy thing. The Japanese call a person who has died *hotoke,* which means "buddha." Under the influence of Christianity, there has also been a recent tendency in Japan for mothers to explain a father's death to children by saying that he has gone to heaven. I hesitate to shatter children's dreams, but according to Buddhism those fathers are almost certainly not in heaven. In Buddhism, death alone cannot make a person a buddha; in all likelihood the dead person would merely be reborn in a hell or as a hungry spirit. To attain enlightenment, and to enter heaven, demands effort and faith.

Non-duality. Non-duality is a concept central to the notion of enlightenment. Non-duality denies all relative and opposite concepts. Only in this denial can the truth appear; it is like a dialectic that resolves opposites. "Neither thought nor non-thought" is an example of non-duality, in that there is a negation of both opposing concepts. In the *Heart Sūtra* (Prajñāpāramitā-hṛdaya-sūtra, ca. 5th–6th century C.E.) the expressions "not born, not destroyed," "not defiled, not pure," and "no ignorance and no end to ignorance" are examples of non-dual thought.

The *Vimalakīrti Sūtra* (Vimalakīrti-nirdeśa-sūtra, trans. into Chinese 5th century) expounds the idea of the non-duality of all existences. The hero of this very popular sūtra is the lay practitioner Vimalakīrti, a man whose deep understanding of the emptiness of transcendental wisdom (*prajñā*) surpasses even that of the ordained disciples of the Buddha. At one point, Vimalakīrti and the disciples discuss the teaching of non-duality. A certain bodhisattva says, "Many wise people think that there is birth and there is death. However, things originally were not born, and therefore they do not die. To enter the gate of non-duality means to gain the tranquillity of mind that comes of the understanding that 'things are not born.'" Other bodhisattvas proceed to deny other opposing concepts, such as pure and defiled, good and evil, and *saṃsāra* ("life and death," "transmigration") and *nirvāṇa* ("eternal peace"). Finally they appeal to the bodhisattva Mañjuśrī, who says, "In my way of thinking, nothing can be said, explained, shown, or discerned about anything at all. Being detached from all questions and answers is to enter the gate of non-duality." Rightly is Mañjuśrī called the embodiment of wisdom! His reply overwhelms the answers of the other bodhisattvas. Then he says to Vimalakīrti, "Everyone has finished. It is now your turn. What is the meaning of entering the gate of non-duality?" But Vimalakīrti says nothing. Mañjuśrī praises him, saying:

"Wonderful, wonderful! You use neither letters nor speech. That indeed is what it truly means to enter the gate of non-duality!"[13]

Non-duality is a philosophy of the absolute. In Buddhism, that which is absolute is true, whereas that which is relative is only temporary, a falsehood. This idea arose from the concept that the world is characterized by suffering, and that we must seek in whatever way we can to remove that suffering. The origin of suffering is believed to be the relativistic nature of the world. Because we discriminate between ourselves and others, pain and anguish arise. This abhorrent world of the relative is not the true world. In the world from which all relativity has been eliminated, that is, the world of the absolute, there is no suffering. That is the realm of truth.

Buddhism gave its whole attention to the question of the nature of the absolute. From the Buddhist point of view, the concept of the absolute in popular usage carried only a faint echo of its true meaning, for it tended to be employed only in the sense of contrasting relative and absolute, not in terms of absolute truth. This distinction is rarely recognized. What do we mean by an absolute god? If we say "an existence standing above all other things," we have not yet understood its meaning sufficiently. We are only comparing "absolute god" with "all things." The true meaning of absolute god is god beyond all concepts of "us" and "god," a god where we and god are one. In this sense, Buddhism is pantheistic.

The idea of a non-dual absolute is not confined to Buddhism. Brahmanism terms the absolute the "identicality of Brahman and Ātman," Brahman being the entire universe, and Ātman the self, real and immortal. The two are, in truth, one. Thinking that the self somehow exists separately from the universe derives from attachment to deluded views created by that very self. The idea of non-duality appears throughout the Brahmanic sacred texts called the *Upaniṣads,* and it is here we should look to discover its origin. It is in the *Bṛhadāraṇyaka-upaniṣad* (Upaniṣad of the Great Forest, 700–500 B.C.E.) that the famous expression *neti, neti* (literally, "not this, not this") appears.

Photo 1. *Stūpa 1 at Sāñcī, in the Indian state of Madhya Pradesh, can be seen as an expression of the Mount Sumeru world. Photo by Isamu Maruyama.*

Photo 2. *Hungry spirits wandering among tombs and eating human remains. Description from the* Gaki Zōshi *("Hungry Spirits Scrolls"). Kawamoto Collection, stored in the Tokyo National Museum.*

Photo 3. *Sculpture of a meditating priest, Mohenjo-Daro, India, from a civilization that flourished around 2300* B.C.E. *Photo by Isamu Maruyama.*

Photo 4. *The fifth-century stūpa in Cave 19, Ajantā, India, is an example of one with a buddha affixed. Photo by Isamu Maruyama.*

Photo 5. *Śākyamuni manifesting himself as a multitude of buddhas in a relief called "Miracle at Śrāvastī," in the Lahore Museum, Pakistan. Photo by Isamu Maruyama.*

Photo 6. *The Great Buddha of Tōdai-ji in Nara, Japan, an image of Vairocana, sits on a pedestal in the shape of a lotus. Photo by Kozo Ogawa.*

Photo 7. *Line carvings on a lotus petal in the throne of the Tōdai-ji Vairocana Buddha. Śākyamuni Buddha and bodhisattvas are depicted, and beneath them are lines segmenting the twenty-five worlds. Photo by Kozo Ogawa.*

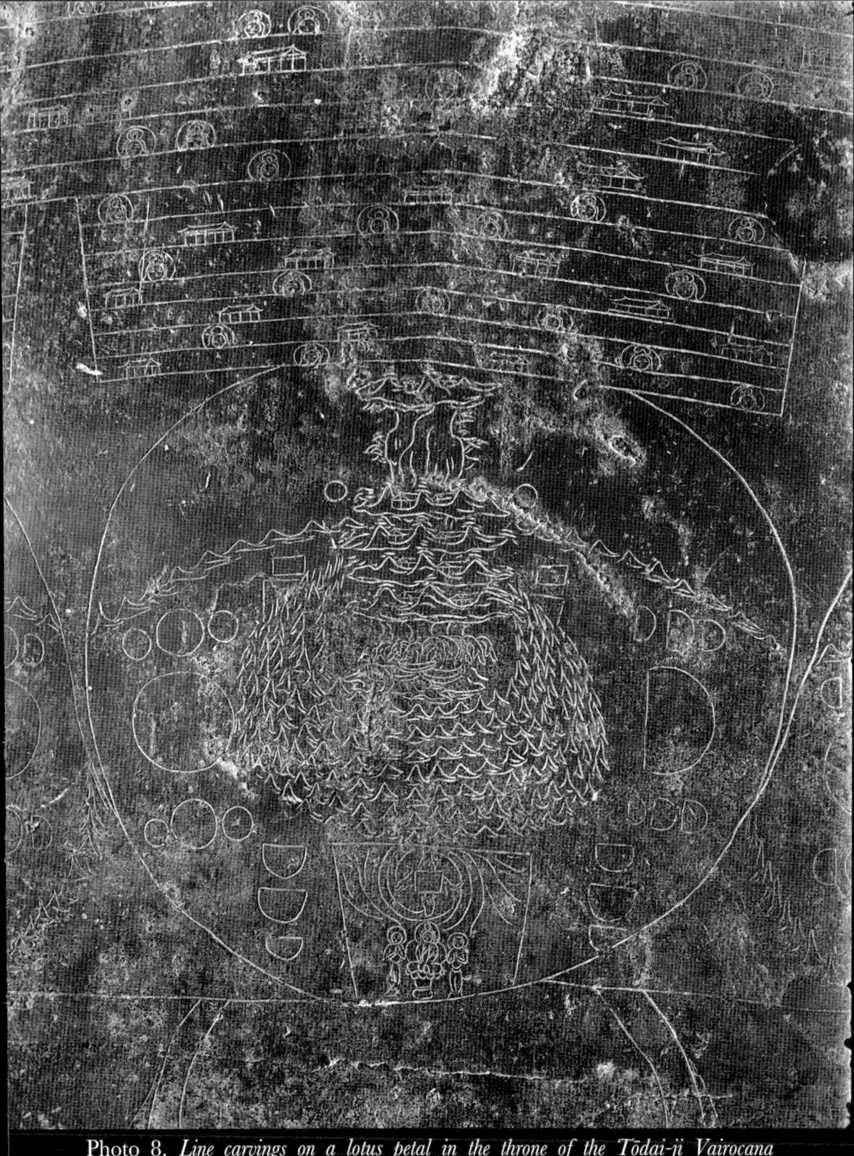

Photo 8. *Line carvings on a lotus petal in the throne of the Tōdai-ji Vairocana Buddha. The Mount Sumeru world shown here is depicted below the twenty-five worlds that also appear in photo 7. Photo by Kozo Ogawa.*

Photo 9. *Meditating Buddha (cosmic Vairocana). Wall painting, probably from Balawaste, Keriya (near Khotan); sixth century* C.E.*; National Museum of India, New Delhi. Photo by Isamu Maruyama.*

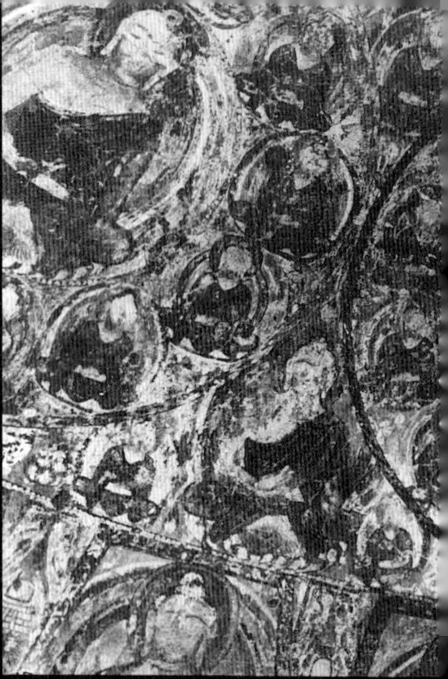

Photo 11. *Wall painting depicting a thousand buddhas in circles, at Bāmiyān, Afghanistan. Reproduced from J. Hackin's* Nouvelles Recherches Archéologiques à Bāmiyān *(MDAFA 3, 1933).*

Photo 10. *Detail from photo 9 showing two-headed snake, and possibly depicting the legend of the Churning of the*

Photo 12. *Cut glass goblet from Begrām, Afghanistan, between first and third centuries.*

Photo 13. *Reconstruction of ornamentation of dome in rock-cut cave XI at Bāmiyān. Reproduced from J. Hackin's* Nouvelles Recherches Archéologiques à Bāmiyān *(MDAFA 3, 1933).*

Photo 14. *Stūpa complex at Borobudur, Indonesia. Photo by PPS.*

The philosopher Yājñavalkya said to his wife Maitreyī:

When there is, as it were, duality, then one sees the other, one smells the other, one tastes the other, one speaks to the other, one hears the other, one perceives the other, one touches the other, one knows the other. But when the one is the self (*ātman*), how should one see another, how should one smell another, how should one taste another, how should one speak to another, how should one hear another, how should one perceive another, how should one touch another, how should one know another? How should one know that through which one knows all this? The self is to be described only as "Not this, not this." It is incomprehensible, for it cannot be comprehended; it is imperishable, for it cannot be destroyed; it is unattached, for it does not attach itself; it is unfettered, for it does not suffer, it does not fail. How should one know the knower? Thus you have already been instructed, O Maitreyī. Ah, immortality is truly thus!

Having said this, Yājñavalkya went away [into the forest].[14]

Those who idealize the absolute tend to be suspicious of what is diverse. Psychologically, their ideal is the absence of discriminatory thought and the cessation of mental functioning. Of the various mental conditions—being awake, being in a dream state, and being deeply asleep—they consider that the first is the condition closest to delusion, for a person who is awake must be in contact with the world at its most diverse. This diversity is reduced somewhat in the dream state, but in the state of deep sleep it disappears entirely. It is when diversity is annihilated that the spirit exists in its purest form.

Yoga. According to Indian tradition, fundamental truth cannot be attained through daily, busy life, but only by the concentrated mind. This concentration of mind is variously called *yoga, samādhi,* or *dhyāna. Yoga* (etymologically the same as the English *yoke*) means "attaching the mind to one object," "concentrating the mind on one thing." *Samādhi* means "putting together (the mind which always tends to disperse)." The Hindu yoga school probably started before the common era, but its most important scripture, the *Yoga-sūtra,* was composed by Patañjali around the fifth century C.E. Many new yogic sects subsequently developed. One of them, Haṭhayoga (*haṭha,* "force, pertinacity") which developed after the twelfth century C.E., specializes in bodily training, in the belief that the body's function and the spirit's function are inseparable.

It is very difficult to probe the origins of this tradition. Among the remains of the Indus Valley civilization that flourished around 2,300 B.C.E., there is a statue excavated from Mohenjo-Daro of a man, perhaps a priest, meditating (see photo 3). His eyes are half-closed, the very image of one who has entered *samādhi* (though some believe that this means only that he is of Mongolian origin). The way his robe is worn over the left shoulder, leaving the right one bare, is similar to the custom that pertained later in Buddhism. (A seal also found at Mohenjo-Daro depicts a man, or perhaps a god, in a yogic pose.) Nevertheless, there is a gap of nearly two thousand years between the Indus Valley civilization and the time of the *Upaniṣads* and the new religious sects. Furthermore, the new religious movements did not arise in the Indus Valley, but in the Ganges Valley. We do not yet know for sure whether this one small statue will be able to bridge the gap of two thousand years and two thousand kilometers.

Yoga is the most non-European of all the ways of thought. European civilization has believed that one can approach reality by seeing things clearly, and that anything else leads to turbidity. For Westerners, lack of cognition is imbecility. In the Yogic teachings about being asleep and awake, however, there is something very persuasive. People often reminisce at the ends of their lives that all has been somehow like a dream. That might very well be true, but it is something that can be fully realized only after we die.

While we dream, we do not doubt the truth of what happens in the dream. After we awake, though, and recall what happened in the dream, we know the dream world to be full of contradictions and impossibilities. In a dream, I can be in one place now and an instant later far away. I can be speaking with someone and then find him turned into someone else. Nevertheless I continue talking, completely unconcerned, and with no doubts whatsoever. To my awakened self, the dream is a world of illusion.

Now I am awake. Things occur logically, leaving no room for doubt. This waking world is not the world of dreams but the realm of undeniable truth. We cannot think otherwise. It is the world of dreams that deceives us, for there not a single doubt arises. But isn't the waking world just the same? It is an even greater trickster. Isn't death itself the true awakening?

4. The Cosmos and Time

In chapter 3 we saw how individual beings transmigrate. According to Buddhism, the cosmos also transmigrates, undergoing drastic changes over long periods of time.

The Thousand-cubed Great-thousand-world

To understand the worldview of Buddhism, it is necessary to comprehend the concept of the thousand-cubed great-thousand-world, or *trichiliocosm*. We begin by examining what a "single world" consists of. The Chinese translation of the *Abhidharmakośa* describes its horizontal limits in the expression, "The Iron Mountains [Cakravāḍa] encircle a single world."[1] A single world thus includes Mount Sumeru, its surrounding mountain ranges and seas, and four landmasses. The vertical boundaries are not as clear, but appear to extend from the circle of wind to Brahmā's world, the First Dhyāna heavens of the realm of form. The heaven of the greatest of all the gods is therefore the upper limit of a single world (see figure 21). The higher *dhyāna* practitioners in the realms of form and of formlessness, and the buddhas, are beyond this world, but all the other five (or six) types of beings dwell in the single world. This world also includes one sun, one moon, and the stars. In modern terms, a single world may equal the solar system.

A thousand single worlds are called a "small-thousand-world." (*Small thousand* means "one thousand.") In modern terms, this would be a galaxy. One thousand small-thousand-worlds make a medium-thousand-world. "Medium-thousand" is *dvi-sāhasra* (literally, "2,000"), a term used to mean $1{,}000^2$, that is, a million worlds. One thousand medium-thousand-worlds make a great-thousand-world. "Great-thousand" (*tri-sāhasra,* literally, "3,000") denotes $1{,}000^3$, that is, one billion worlds. A great-thousand-world is also called a "thousand-cubed great-thousand-world" (*tri-sāhasra-mahāsāhasro loka-dhātuḥ*), or *trichiliocosm.* These worlds all experience the Buddhist cycle of existence and disappearance together, so they can be called a single unit in terms of destiny.

The upper three Dhyāna stages in the realm of form and the stages of the realm of formlessness are not included in the *trichiliocosm,* but it is incorrect to say that they transcend space and time. The Second, Third, and Fourth Dhyānas' heavens have physical limits, and the living beings who inhabit them have specific life spans. In contrast, the realm of formlessness is without size, transcending spatial dimensions. It is not, however, beyond the reach of time, and its inhabitants also follow allotted life spans. (In the abode of the infinity of space their life span is twenty thousand great *kalpas,* in the abode of the infinity of consciousness it is forty thousand great *kalpas,* in the abode of nothingness it is sixty thousand great *kalpas,* and in the abode of neither thought nor non-thought, eighty thousand great *kalpas.*)

The *Abhidharmakośa* does not mention multiples of the upper three Dhyāna stages, but other sūtras and commentaries suggest such plurality.[2] A small-thousand-world includes one thousand suns and one thousand Brahmā heavens, whereas a medium-thousand-world has a million suns, a million Brahmā heavens, and also one thousand Second Dhyāna heavens. A great-thousand-world has a billion suns, and a billion Brahmā heavens, a million Second Dhyāna heavens, and a thousand Third Dhyāna heavens.

TIME, SEASONS, AND HUMAN LIFE

Time. The concept of the trichiliocosm is closely linked with Buddhist theories about time and human destiny. Buddhist thought is generally clouded with pessimism, and this is nowhere more obvious than in its concept of time. The notion of an eternal round of birth and death is an intolerable thought. I will discuss this further, but would first like to introduce some basic units of time and discuss time in terms of daily life.

In ascending order, the basic units of time are:

kṣaṇa (1/75 second)
tat-kṣaṇa; equals 120 *kṣaṇas* (1 3/5 seconds)
lava; equals 60 *tat-kṣaṇas* (1 minute 36 seconds)
muhūrta; equals 30 *lavas* (48 minutes)
aho-rātra; equals 30 *muhūrtas* (24 hours, day)
māsa; equals 30 *aho-rātra*s (month)
saṃvatsara (year)

Thus a *muhūrta* more or less corresponds to an hour, a *lava* to a minute, and a *tat-kṣaṇa* to a second. A *kṣaṇa* represents a very tiny unit of time, for which we do not possess any modern unit.

There is another way to explain a *kṣaṇa*'s small size. A *kṣaṇa* is the time it takes "for a dharma to arise when all the causes and conditions have come together," that is, for a certain existence, thing, or being to emerge when all the conditions are in place.[3] Certain chemical compounds, for example, suddenly form when the temperature is right. The *Great Commentary* graphically describes the brevity of a *kṣaṇa:* "Two adult men stretch tight a big cable of Kāśī silk thread. Another adult man severs that cable in one stroke with a strong Chinese blade. The time the blade takes to pass through one thread is sixty-four *kṣaṇas*."[4] Silk from Kāśī seems to have been extremely fine, and the cable would consist of hundreds or thousands of threads. The blade takes perhaps 64,000 *kṣaṇas* to pass through the whole cable, and that is one stroke by an adult man! You can imagine how brief a unit the *kṣaṇa* is.

Now let us examine units longer than a day. A month consists of thirty *aho-rātras* ("days and nights"), but there were also six months with only twenty-nine. The Indians knew that a month actually has about twenty-nine and a half days. Modern astronomy has accurately calculated the time of a synodical month (from one full moon to the next) as being an average of 29 days, 12 hours, 44 minutes, and 2.8 seconds.

A year consists of twelve such months ($30 \times 6 + 29 \times 6 = 354$ days). In the *Abhidharmakośa,* time units finish with "year" (*saṃvatsara*). There is, however, another enormous unit of time that we could add, the *kalpa,* which is so long that it cannot be calculated in years. (The Chinese transliterated *kalpa* as *kiap* and translated it as "great time." In the Japanese game of Go there is a rule known as *kō* [Japanese for *kiap*] to prevent stalemates through constant repetition. Without it, the game could continue indefinitely.)

Buddhist writings demonstrate the length of a *kalpa* by a number of similes. It is at least the time required to take away all the mustard seeds stored in a castle of one cubic *yojana* (7.4 cubic kilometers) if only one seed is removed every hundred years. Alternatively, it is at least the time taken to wear away a great rock of one cubic *yojana* by wiping it with a piece of soft cotton (*karpāsa*) from Kāśī once every hundred years. These similes are found in the *Miscellaneous Discourses* (Saṃyuktāgama, date uncertain, probably 3d century B.C.E.–1st century C.E.). Some sūtras substitute the robe of a celestial woman (which is extremely soft) for the piece of Kāśī cotton.

This immense amount of time is still short compared with the "great *kalpa*" (*mahākalpa*) and the cycle of sixty-four great *kalpas*. One great *kalpa* consists of eighty *kalpas*. (When comparing a *kalpa* with a great *kalpa,* we usually call the original *kalpa* an "intermediate *kalpa*" [*antarakalpa*].) A great *kalpa* is truly an enormous length of time, and sixty-four are immeasurably longer, of course. This should not occasion surprise, however, for there exists even a vaster amount of time, the *asaṃkhya kalpa,* in comparison with which these seem no more than brief moments. *Asaṃkhya* has often been mistranslated as "infinite," but actually it is a number representing 10 to the power of 59. Three *asaṃkhya kalpas,* the time deemed necessary to train to become a buddha, is therefore 3×10^{59}. Some commentaries say the *kalpas* spoken of here are great *kalpas,* and others say they are intermediate *kalpas.*

Seasonal changes and the calendar. The day, month, and year are closely connected to everyday life, and regulate its rhythms. Buddhist priests used the lunar calendar, which began and ended with the full moon. The first half of the month (Kṛṣṇapakṣa) was the period from the full moon to the new moon, and the second half (Śuklapakṣa), the period from the new moon to the full moon. Kṛṣṇapakṣa (black half), the period of the darkening or waning moon, was the time when there was little moon in the sky (or perhaps the time when the moon rose late at night). Śuklapakṣa (bright half) was the time when the moon could be seen in the sky during the evening. With the month divided into two halves this way, the priests would count the days as the fourth day of Kṛṣṇapakṣa or the fifteenth day of Śuklapakṣa, rather than as the sixteenth or the thirtieth of the month. To be precise, however, there were some months when the first part (Kṛṣṇapakṣa) had only fourteen days. At such times the month would be a "small" month of twenty-nine days, rather than a "large" month of thirty days. Small and large months alternated. This was a natural result, because the synodical month is about twenty-nine and a half days. The months were named for constellations. Thus if the full moon of a particular month arose in the Pleiades (Kṛttikā) the month was named Kārttika.

So far we have seen how the moon's cycle governed the construction of the calendar. India has seasonal changes, however, which are cyclical and based on the sun's movement. Buddhists recognized three seasons, calling them the "cold season" (*hemanta*), "hot season" (*grīṣma*), and "rainy season" (*varṣa*). Indians who were not Buddhists, on the other hand, had six seasons, "advancing heat" (*vasanta*), "great heat" (*grīṣma*), "rainy season" (*varṣa*), "dry season" or "season of ripening" (*śarad*), "advancing cold" (*hemanta*), and "great cold" (*śiśira*).

Let us now examine how the lunar and solar cycles were connected. Hsüan-tsang (600–662 C.E.) mentions that the first season of the year was not the "cold season," but instead the "hot season." He adds the divisions of spring, summer, autumn, and winter to the divisions of three or six seasons. This concept of four seasons is vague, however, in view of India's climate, and it is uncertain whether it was generally used. The information in the relevant passage from Hsüan-tsang's *Records of the Western Regions of the Great T'ang Dynasty* is tabulated in figure 22, together with Gregorian calendar months.

It is of interest to see how the Indian months match our own months, which are based on the solar calendar. The *Abhidharmakośa* says, "The nights lengthen after the ninth day of the latter half of the second month during the rainy season."[5] The second month of the rainy season is the sixth in the table, Bhādrapada. The ninth day of the latter half of the month is the ninth day of Śuklapakṣa, which means, in our way of counting, the twenty-third day of Bhādrapada. It is not certain whether "lengthening of the nights" refers to the phenomenon that begins in the summer solstice or in the autumn equinox. At any rate, it seems unreasonable to think that the phenomenon begins in Bhādrapada, because in those days, Caitra was the month that contained the spring equinox, as in figure 22.[6]

There appears to be a considerable discrepancy between the Indian months and our own; the lunar calendar shifts between a half and one month every two or three years. It is only natural that the information in the *Abhidharmakośa* (5th century C.E.) and *Records of the Western Regions* (7th century C.E.) should not completely accord with our calendar. Neither work mentions what Buddhists thought about the discrepancies between the solar and lunar calendars, but there is little doubt that intercalary months were inserted when necessary. Three years of twelve months (354 days) would result in a discrepancy of about a month in comparison with the solar calendar. This would mean that Caitra, now at the beginning of the hot season, would in three years be at the end of the cold season.

For Buddhist priests, the pure lunar calendar might have been preferred, in order to preserve the rhythm of religious life. The important meeting of members of the order, called *uposatha* in Pāli (*upavasatha* in Sanskrit), was held regularly at full moon, new moon, and days in the middle of each interval between full and new. *Māsa* ("month") derives from the Indo-European root *mā* ("to measure"). For priests, the month was the most convenient measure of time. For farmers, however, the sun would have been the most important indicator.

The very important rainy season retreat (*vārṣika* in Sanskrit), however, could not ignore the changing seasons. Religious practitioners remained in one place during the three-month period of heavy rains, which lasted either from Śrāvaṇa to Aśvayuja or from Bhādrapada to Kārttika, depending on differences in climate, calendar, and location. In linking the names of the months to the period of the rainy season retreat, Buddhist priests almost certainly calculated the retreat through a system of intercalary months that was common throughout India.

This discussion must seem unexpectedly down-to-earth after the cosmological flights of imagination we have seen in earlier chapters. At times, such realism does appear in the fanciful Buddhist scheme, for Buddhists themselves could not escape the practicalities of daily life.

THE CYCLE OF INCREASE AND DECREASE OF THE UNIVERSE

The cycle of four periods. The universe, with its multiple worlds and variety of living beings, eternally repeats a cycle of fourfold change (see figure 23). Each of the four periods lasts twenty intermediate *kalpas,* so one complete cycle takes eighty intermediate *kalpas.* The cycle includes the *Kalpa* of Dissolution

INDIAN CALENDAR

<table>
<tr><th></th><th></th><th>Three seasons</th><th>Six seasons (ṛtu)</th><th>Four seasons</th></tr>
<tr><td>1. Caitra</td><td>Kṛṣṇapakṣa
Śuklapakṣa</td><td rowspan="4">hot
(grīṣma)</td><td rowspan="2">advancing heat
(vasanta)</td><td rowspan="3">spring</td></tr>
<tr><td>2. Vaiśākha</td><td>Kṛṣṇapakṣa*
Śuklapakṣa</td></tr>
<tr><td>3. Jyaiṣṭha</td><td>Kṛṣṇapakṣa
Śuklapakṣa</td><td rowspan="2">great heat
(grīṣma)</td></tr>
<tr><td>4. Āṣāḍha</td><td>Kṛṣṇapakṣa*
Śuklapakṣa</td><td rowspan="3">summer</td></tr>
<tr><td>5. Śrāvaṇa</td><td>Kṛṣṇapakṣa
Śuklapakṣa</td><td rowspan="4">rainy
(varṣa)</td><td rowspan="2">rainy season
(varṣa)</td></tr>
<tr><td>6. Bhādrapada</td><td>Kṛṣṇapakṣa*
Śuklapakṣa</td></tr>
<tr><td>7. Aśvayuja</td><td>Kṛṣṇapakṣa
Śuklapakṣa</td><td rowspan="2">dry season
(śarad)</td><td rowspan="3">autumn</td></tr>
<tr><td>8. Kārttika</td><td>Kṛṣṇapakṣa*
Śuklapakṣa</td></tr>
<tr><td>9. Mārgaśiras</td><td>Kṛṣṇapakṣa
Śuklapakṣa</td><td rowspan="4">cold
(hemanta)</td><td rowspan="2">advancing cold
(hemanta)</td></tr>
<tr><td>10. Pauṣa</td><td>Kṛṣṇapakṣa*
Śuklapakṣa</td><td rowspan="3">winter</td></tr>
<tr><td>11. Māgha</td><td>Kṛṣṇapakṣa
Śuklapakṣa</td><td rowspan="2">great cold
(śiśira)</td></tr>
<tr><td>12. Phālguna</td><td>Kṛṣṇapakṣa*
Śuklapakṣa</td></tr>
</table>

Fig. 22. Comparison of Indian, Chinese, and Gregorian Calendars
Under the Chinese calendar are listed first the month according to Hsüan-tsang, and the correct month in parentheses. (* These half-months have only 14 days.)

CHINESE CALENDAR		GREGORIAN CALENDAR
1st month (2d month)	spring equinox	March
2d month (3d month)		April
3d month (4th month)		May
4th month (5th month)		June
5th month (6th month)		July
6th month (7th month)		August
7th month (8th month)		September
8th month (9th month)		October
9th month (10th month)		November
10th month (11th month)		December
11th month (12th month)		January
12th month (1st month)		February
1st month (2d month)		March

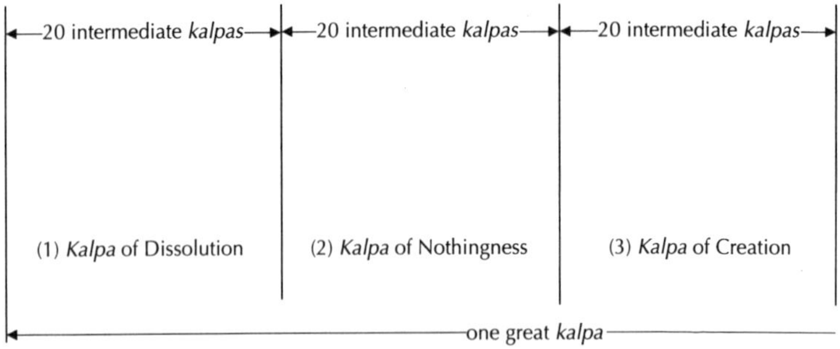

Fig. 23. Cycle of the Universe

(Saṃvartakalpa); the *Kalpa* of Nothingness (Saṃvartasthāyikalpa), during which the world remains dissolved; the *Kalpa* of Creation (Vivartakalpa); and the *Kalpa* of Duration of the created world (Vivartasthāyikalpa). That the cycle starts with dissolution is a very Indian way of thinking, as is the custom of calculating the month from the full moon.

The *Kalpa* of Dissolution begins when beings are no longer reborn in the hells. When all living beings disappear from the hells, the hells themselves vanish. The process is repeated in the abodes of hungry spirits and animals. As for human beings, when one person is reborn in a First Dhyāna heaven and experiences the joy brought about by abandonment of evil life, that motivates all others to enter *samādhi* and be reborn there. Likewise, among *devas* of the First Dhyāna heavens, when one of their number is reborn in a Second Dhyāna heaven and experiences the joy resulting from *samādhi*, all the others receive an impetus to enter *samādhi* and be reborn there. When the karma of living beings that created the world is finally exhausted (because there are no more living beings in the world), seven suns appear and burn up the wind circle, water circle, golden earth layer, Mount Sumeru, the four landmasses, and the Brahmā palace at the highest point of the First Dhyāna heavens. Beings who escaped,

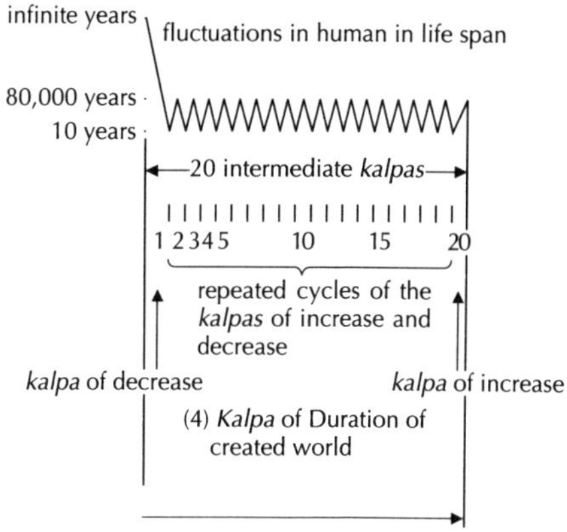

so to speak, to the Second Dhyāna heavens can evade this catastrophe.

When the hells and the abodes of the hungry spirits and animals finally disappear, evil ones living in the human world might clap their hands in glee, saying, "Now I can do anything I want to. There is now no longer any place below the human realm to which I can fall." Similarly, those who entered the hells just before their final dissolution would no doubt rejoice that their period of torment would be very short. Their joy would be premature, however. The *Abhidharmakośa* says that the inhabitants of hells who have not yet received their full measure of punishment would be transferred by the force of their karma to a hell in another universe.

Next comes the *Kalpa* of Nothingness, in which the world remains dissolved for twenty intermediate *kalpas*.

The *Kalpa* of Creation begins when a tiny wind begins to blow "through the indirect force of the karma of living beings" (who and where these living beings are is not clear). The wind circle forms, then the water circle, the golden earth layer, the soil, the four landmasses, and Mount Sumeru. The palaces and abodes reappear exactly as they were before, peopled by the rebirth in lower realms of those who had escaped to the Second Dhyāna heavens at the time of the period of dissolution. Some beings are born in the Brahmā palaces in the highest First Dhyāna heaven, some in the lower Para-nirmita-vaśavartin and Nirmāṇa-rati heavens and other heavens of the realm of desire, some in Pūrvavideha, Jambudvīpa, Aparagodānīya, or Uttarakuru, and some in the lower realms—those of animals or hungry spirits, or hell. When the universe has been thus filled from top to bottom with living beings, the *Kalpa* of Creation ends. During this time, the human life span is "infinite."

During the *Kalpa* of Duration, all those who came into being during the previous period simply continue to exist. Now there are changes in the human life span. During the first intermediate *kalpa,* the life span gradually decreases from the initial "infinite" number of years to 10 years. This is called the *kalpa* of decrease. In the second intermediate *kalpa* the process reverses, and the life span gradually increases to 80,000 years before diminishing again to 10 years. This is called the *kalpa* of increase and decrease. The pattern of the second *kalpa* is repeated throughout the third to the nineteenth intermediate *kalpas*. During the twentieth intermediate *kalpa* the life span, which was 10 years at the end of the nineteenth intermediate *kalpa,* increases again to 80,000 years. This is called the *kalpa* of increase (see figure 23).

Another distinctive feature of the *Kalpa* of Duration is that during it there occur the "three small catastrophes"—war, pestilence, and famine. Two theories exist as to the exact time of their occurrence. The first is that at the end of each intermediate *kalpa,* when the human life span is 10 years, they come one after the other. War continues for seven days and nights. Pestilence follows the end of war and lasts for seven months plus seven days and nights. After this comes famine, for seven years, seven months, and seven days and nights. The second theory says that only one kind of catastrophe will occur in each intermediate *kalpa.* Thus, in the first intermediate *kalpa,* when the human life span is 10 years, pestilence arises; at the same time in the second intermediate *kalpa,* the fires of war occur; and at that point in the third intermediate *kalpa,* famine comes. This pattern continues throughout the intermediate *kalpas,* and each catastrophe lasts for seven days. According to this theory, we are now in the ninth intermediate *kalpa,* a time of decreasing life span, when a great famine will occur.

In this way the universe follows the cycle of dissolution, nothingness, creation, and duration of what is created. The length of one such cycle (eighty intermediate *kalpas*) is called a "great *kalpa*" (*mahākalpa*). The realms that undergo this cycle through one great *kalpa* are the First Dhyāna heavens (the heaven of Mahābrahmā) and those below.[7] Can we therefore assume that the inhabitants of the Second Dhyāna heavens and above are safe? By no means so. Figure 24 shows the relationship between the "three great catastrophes" (*saṃvartanīs*) of fire, water, and wind that destroy the world and the cycle of sixty-four great *kalpas.* Each great *kalpa,* the universe is destroyed by fire caused by the seven suns. Every eighth great *kalpa* a more fearful flood destroys the universe and consumes all abodes up to and including the Second Dhyāna heavens. When the universe has been destroyed seven times by water, it is brought to an end the next time by wind, which causes the destruction of all the abodes up to and including the Third Dhyāna heavens. This occurs once every sixty-four great *kalpas,* which forms one great cycle of destruction. Only those beings that dwell within the Fourth Dhyāna heavens or one of the heavens of the realm of formlessness, therefore, are safe.

Human life and appearance of buddhas. According to Buddhism, the human life span today has diminished to around a hundred years, and will continue to decrease. That we are living in a time of increasing evil is a common idea among ancient people. Hinduism, for instance, recognizes four ages (*catur-yuga*) of the world: Kṛta (gold, lasting 1,728,000 years), Tretā (silver, lasting 1,296,000 years), Dvāpara (brass, lasting 864,000 years), and

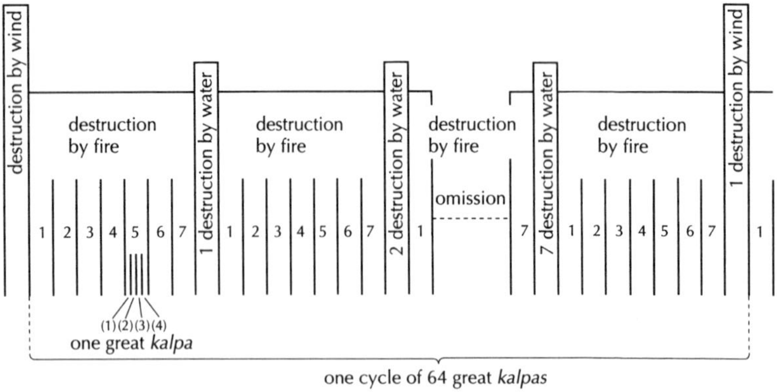

Fig. 24. Relationship of the Three Great Catastrophes to the Cycle of Sixty-Four Great *Kalpas*
(1) *Kalpa* of Dissolution, (2) *Kalpa* of Nothingness, (3) *Kalpa* of Creation, and (4) *Kalpa* of Duration of the created universe

Kali (iron, lasting 432,000 years). This cycle continues infinitely. We are living in the Kali-yuga, the most inferior of the four ages. (According to the Arab scholar and scientist Al-Bīrūnī [973–1048 C.E.], the Kali-yuga began on February 18, 3102 B.C.E.) The ancient Greeks also divided time symbolically into gold, silver, copper, and iron.

The Buddhist idea of the period of the Decay of the Dharma is similar to these philosophies about the ages. According to Buddhist theory, the Buddha's teachings degenerate over three periods. These are called the period of the True Dharma, when teaching, practice, and attainment of emancipation are all possible; the period of the Counterfeit Dharma, when only teaching and practice of Buddhism remain and emancipation is impossible; and the period of the Decay of the Dharma, when only the Buddhist teachings survive. One theory states that the first period lasted five hundred years after the death of Śākyamuni and the second, one thousand years, whereas the third will continue for ten thousand years. Another theory makes the first and second periods last one thousand years and the third, ten thousand.

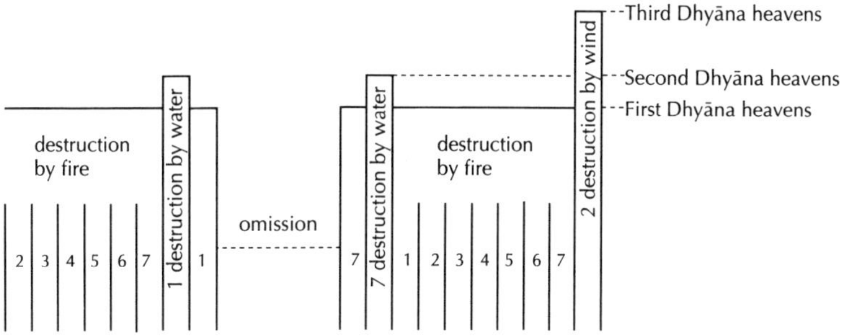

Śākyamuni died in the fifth or fourth century B.C.E. Soon after that, it seems that his teachings were in danger of abandonment, and this filled his followers with a sense of crisis. Perhaps this gave rise to the idea of the three periods of the teachings. Those who established the theory maintained vigorously that their age had already entered the time of weakening (second period) or degeneration (third period). To prove they had already entered the period of the Decay of the Dharma, they manipulated the timing of the three periods to agree with the difference between their own time and the Buddha's death. These notions, of living in an increasingly evil age and of the periodic occurrence of catastrophes in the universe, seem to give Buddhist cosmology a pessimistic tone. But it is exactly because of this that Buddhism maintains the need for salvation and teaches that buddhas appear regularly in the universe for this purpose.

A buddha can appear only during the *kalpa* of decrease within the *Kalpa* of Duration, when the human life span is between 80,000 and 100 years. Buddhas do not appear during *kalpas* of increase, for then human beings are living longer and longer in a prosperous world, so they are content and in no frame of mind to listen to a buddha's teachings. Nor do they appear when the life span has sunk to between 100 and 10 years, for then human beings have become so inferior that they lack the ability to respond to the teachings. This is a time called the "evil world," permeated by five corruptions (*kaṣāyas*): the "corruption of life" (*āyuṣ-kaṣāya*), because the human life span is short; the "corruption of the *kalpa*" (*kalpa-kaṣāya*), because the natural environment worsens; the "corruption of the passions" (*kleśa-kaṣāya*), because beings pursue only pleasure; the "corruption of views" (*dṛṣṭi-kaṣāya*), because religious practitioners pursue false opinions; and the "corruption of living beings" (*sattva-kaṣāya*), because beings are physically and mentally inferior.

A buddha does not appear in every *kalpa* of decrease. As the expression "one universe, one buddha" seems to indicate, a buddha will appear only once in the course of a great *kalpa*, which is one cycle of dissolution, nothingness, creation, and duration. During a great *kalpa*, the period of decrease between 80,000 and 100 years occurs nineteen times (this refers to the first nineteen of the twenty intermediate *kalpas* in the *Kalpa* of Duration), and a buddha may appear in only one of them. We have been born as humans in the intermediate *kalpa* that has seen the appearance of Śākyamuni. Because he lived for only 80 years, we are able to come into contact with him only through his teachings. But even this is a great thing.

In this sense, Buddhists consider a personal encounter with a buddha a rare chance, and an occasion for deep gratitude. The rarity of this opportunity is emphasized by the Buddhist saying that it is as difficult for a living being to be born human and to encounter the Buddha as for a blind turtle that raises its head above the surface of the sea only once in a hundred years to put its head in a hole in a floating log. This metaphor encourages the devotee to pursue religious training.

According to the theory of the Auspicious *Kalpa,* many more buddhas are expected to appear.[8] This theory divides time into three *kalpas,* the past *Kalpa* of Adornment, the present Auspicious *Kalpa,* and the future *Kalpa* of Constellations, in each of which a thousand buddhas appear. Sūtras listing the names of the thousand buddhas of each *kalpa* were composed.[9] It is not clear what connection these three *kalpas* have with the *kalpas* discussed above (the *Abhidharmakośa* does not mention them), but it appears that the Auspicious *Kalpa* of the present is considered identical with the *Kalpa* of Duration.[10] Here, then, we have not just one buddha appearing in the *Kalpa* of Duration, but one thousand.

In northwest India around the third century C.E., the belief grew that Maitreya would be the next buddha, following Śākyamuni. At present accumulating religious training as a bodhisattva, Maitreya is the focus of hope of those born too late to enjoy Śākyamuni's salvation. All the same, he is not due to appear until 5,670,000,000 years after Śākyamuni's death.[11]

Reflecting on the description of the universe presented in the last four chapters, the reader will be aware that much of Buddhist cosmology seems fantastical. The physical layout of the cosmos has a logic mostly unrelated to what we know of the universe, and the mathematical calculations consist of apparently arbitrary numbers which, however, are strangely precise. Naturally, ideas such as the centrality of the Indian experience to the cosmology and the existence of hells inside the earth do not hold true today. All the same, we do not necessarily gain by interpreting Buddhist cosmology purely in terms of geography and revealing all its deficiencies, for to a certain extent it was constructed as a symbolic representation. For example, we may infer that the authors of the cosmology depicted it symbolically from the first, given the overly schematic description of the universe and the too-artificial numbers of the worlds' dimensions. Of course those authors did not come out and say that their cosmology was symbolic. Because of the boldness of expression, though, both speakers and hearers must have understood it as being so. If we comprehend it in this way, we can appreciate the sophistication of ancient Buddhist cosmology. It explained graphically, in a way that is easy to memorize, the entire picture of the world and the universe. In this sense it is of little import that the individual numbers and configurations do not match reality.

PART TWO
Mahāyāna Cosmology

5. The Western Pure Land

So far we have been discussing Buddhist cosmology largely in terms of the *Abhidharmakośa.* This we might call for convenience the classical view, a product of a time when Buddhism was organizationally at its most stable. The cosmology that we are about to examine, in contrast, is the product of new doctrinal developments which occurred with the segmentation of Buddhism and the rise of Mahāyāna thinking. While in Hīnayāna Buddhism the Buddha appears and disappears in the universe, in Mahāyāna thought the Buddha is the universe itself, eternal existence. This idea was probably influenced by the notion of Brahmā, Brahmanism's fundamental principle of the universe, and by Hinduism's concept of the gods Viṣṇu and Śiva.

Mahāyāna Buddhism arose in India around the first century C.E. It can be classified into three periods: early, or dynamic (1st century C.E. to 4th century C.E.), middle, or scholastic (4th–mid-7th century), and late, or esoteric (mid-7th–early 13th century).

SAHĀ AND SUKHĀVATĪ

In the *Abhidharmakośa,* despite all that was written about hells and heavens, there is not one word about the key Mahāyāna idea of *Sukhāvatī* ("supreme joy"). To understand this concept, let us first take a brief look at the Mahāyāna notion of the Sahā world. *Sahā* refers to the world in which we live, the stage for Śākyamuni's appearance and the object of his teaching. *Sahā,* "a place where suffering is endured," (and its variant *Sabhā,* "confused congregation") appears to derive from the Sanskrit word *sabhaya,* meaning "a land of fear." All these words describe this world as a realm of defilements, filled with suffering.

There are a number of different opinions concerning the extent of Sahā; some say it is Jambudvīpa, some say it comprises the four landmasses, and some say that it is a thousand-cubed great-thousand-world. Hsüan-tsang defines Sahā as the thousand-cubed great-thousand-world that is the object of the teaching of one buddha. The *Perfection of Wisdom Sūtra in 25,000 Verses* (Fang-kuang pan-jo-ching, ca. 1st century C.E.) says, "In the far limits of the west is a world called Sahā, whose buddha is named Śākyamuni."[1] The *Smaller Sukhāvatī-vyūha* (Amitābha sūtra, ca. 1st century C.E.) says: "Śākyamuni Buddha did those things that are extremely difficult and rare; [that is,] he did attain Perfect Enlightenment in the Sahā world, the evil world, permeated by the five corruptions."[2]

Let us now turn our attention to the Mahāyāna expression *buddha-realm* or *buddha-land.* Mahāyāna thought posits not just one buddha, but many buddhas throughout the universe. (Chapter 6 describes the origins and characteristics of these buddhas in more detail.) They possess their own lands, apart from the Sahā world, in which they teach. These are called *buddha-lands, buddha-realms,* or *pure lands.* Best known are the Realm of Profound Joy of Akṣobhya Buddha, the Pure Lapis-lazuli World of Bhaiṣajya-guru Buddha, and the Pure Land of Sukhāvatī of Amida (Amitābha/Amitāyus). Resembling buddha-lands, though not strictly identical, is the Tuṣita heaven, one of the six heavens of the realm of desire and the dwelling place of bodhisattvas prior to their appearance on earth as buddhas. Śākyamuni descended to Jambudvīpa from there, and at present Maitreya, the future buddha, lives there. Another place resembling buddha-lands is Mount Potalaka, said to be located in the sea south of India, where Avalokiteśvara Bodhisattva dwells. The Sahā world might seem to be the buddha-land of Śākyamuni; it is not, however, a "pure land," but rather a defiled realm, and thus is quite distinct from the buddha-lands. Śākyamuni, moreover, is a historical person and other buddhas are mythological or metaphysical beings.

In the pre-Mahāyāna *Abhidharmakośa,* the Buddha is described as gaining liberation from the three realms of desire, form, and formlessness and returning to nothingness. Such a return to complete nothingness (termed *nirupadhiśeṣa-nirvāṇa,* "nirvāṇa without residue") was the goal of pre-Mahāyāna Buddhists. They had no concept of a buddha that retains form and is active in a buddha-land. In Mahāyāna Buddhism, though, the buddhas resolve to train themselves to build their own buddha-lands and work eternally to bring to those lands all the living beings now lost in delusion. We of Sahā can be reborn virtually only in Sukhāvatī, because Amitābha is the only buddha who offers us an effective means for rebirth there (i.e., *nembutsu,* calling upon Amitābha). Though Śākyamuni and Amitābha have completely different origins, the Pure Land sūtras depict Śākyamuni as expounding Amitābha's teachings.

There are two theories concerning the location of Amitābha Buddha's pure land of Sukhāvatī. One places it within the three realms, and the other places it outside them. The reason for this division of opinion lies in the fact that classical cosmology did not speak of buddha-lands. All agree, however, that Sukhāvatī is "ten myriads of a hundred millions of buddha-lands to the west of Sahā," an expression found in the Chinese translations of the *Smaller* and *Larger Sukhāvatī-vyūha* sūtras. Thus another name for Sukhāvatī is the Western Pure Land. Specific distances and directions are also given for other pure lands. The Realm of Profound Joy is one thousand buddha-lands to the east of Sahā, the Pure Lapis-lazuli World lies to the east by ten times the number of buddha-lands equaling the sands of the Ganges, and the Unconquerable World of the Buddha Śākyamuni (perhaps the same Śākyamuni as the buddha of the Sahā world) is to the west by forty-two times the number of buddha-lands equaling the sands of the Ganges. Because of discrepancies between the Sanskrit and Chinese versions of certain sūtras, we cannot accurately interpret the extent of a buddha-land itself. All we can say with confidence is that the distance between Sahā and Sukhāvatī, "ten myriads of a hundred millions of buddha-lands," is indeed vast.[3]

As the Chinese translation of the name *Sukhāvatī* suggests, it is a land of supreme joy. The Sanskrit is of similar meaning: "that which possesses ease and comfort." Sukhāvatī is not subject to the sufferings that plague this world and, furthermore, it is a land of unsurpassed beauty. It is described as having seven tiers of balustrades, seven rows of nets, and seven rows of trees, all adorned with the four jewels (gold, silver, lapis lazuli, and crystal). There is a lake of the seven jewels (gold, silver, lapis lazuli, crystal, a kind of a big shell [*tridacna gigas*], coral, and agate), filled with water having the eight virtues. The bottom of the lake is gold sand. On the four sides of the lake are stairs (galleries) made of the four jewels. Above are towers and palaces also adorned with the seven jewels. In the lake bloom lotus flowers as large as chariot wheels. The blue lotus flowers emit a blue light, and the yellow, red, and white lotus flowers emit light of corresponding colors. They all give forth a sweet fragrance.

The delightful sound of heavenly music can be heard, and in the morning, at noon, and in the evening mandārava flowers fall from the sky and gently pile up on the golden ground. Every morning the inhabitants of the Pure Land gather these flowers with the hems of their robes and make offerings of them to myriads of buddhas in other lands. At mealtime they return to their own land, where they take their meal and stroll around.

There are many kinds of birds—swans, peacocks, parrots, sharikas, kalaviṅkas, and jīvaṃjīvakas, which sing with beautiful voices, proclaiming the teachings of the Buddha. When living beings hear this song, they think about the Buddha, Dharma ("law," or his teachings), and Saṅgha ("community of believers"). When the gentle breezes blow, the rows of four-jeweled trees and jeweled nets give forth a gentle music, like a beautiful symphony.

In this land dwell Amitābha Buddha and his two attendants,

the bodhisattvas Avalokiteśvara and Mahāsthāmaprāpta. At their feet are those virtuous beings who have been reborn in that land because of their ardent faith. All, however, are male; women of deep faith are reborn here with male bodies. The female sex, considered inferior and unfortunate, has no place in Sukhāvatī.

All people, says Śākyamuni, should ardently wish for rebirth in that land and become the companions of the most virtuous of all beings. People cannot hope for rebirth there just by performing a few good deeds, however. If living beings meditate eagerly upon the name of Amitābha for even one day with an undisturbed mind, Amitābha and his holy retinue will appear before them to receive them at the end of life. They will enter the Pure Land with unperturbed hearts.

It is obvious that the concept of Sukhāvatī is related to the senses, not to ethics. The court nobility of the Heian period (794–1185 C.E.) in Japan, whose yearning after the beauty of Sukhāvatī was expressed in such forms as the lotus pond of Byōdō-in at Uji, Kyoto, and the Taima Mandala (a depiction of the Pure Land made of lotus threads) at Taima-ji, harbored no dissatisfaction with this type of land. Modern religious seekers, though, probably would feel that this description lacks profundity. Others might feel disappointed that they cannot find female companions. One point in favor of Sukhāvatī's sensuous character is the fact that a purely spiritual realm is unhealthy and difficult to bear. In regard to the lack of women, the male priests did not consider womanhood a pleasurable state, and thus could only provide for the happiness of women through conversion to male form.

The idea of Sukhāvatī certainly grew out of the concept of a material paradise, but early on it became allied with an elevated spiritual and ethical outlook, the teaching of the Buddha as rescuer, in which Amitābha Buddha, lord of Sukhāvatī, saves those who meditate upon him. Classical Buddhism taught that salvation must occur by one's own efforts ("self-power"). Those who had lost hope in salvation through their own efforts flocked to the new teaching of salvation through the power of another, i.e., of Amitābha Buddha.

At first, people attracted to this new teaching were probably motivated by a desire to escape from suffering into what was conceived of as a materially satisfying land. But Sukhāvatī was soon linked with the idea of good and evil, and those who sought to be reborn in Sukhāvatī did so out of despair at their own evil. A good example of such a thinker is Shinran (1173–1262 C.E.), the Japanese priest who founded the True Pure Land (Jōdo Shin) sect. Modern Pure Land thought resembles Christianity in many ways—the strong monotheistic coloration, salvation through the Buddha (God), the concern with good and evil rather than with suffering and pleasure. In the mid-twentieth century, Kamegai Ryōun, a Jōdo Shin sect priest, converted to Christianity on the grounds that the Jōdo Shin sect was preparing the road leading to Christianity. It certainly seems possible that in its two thousand years, Pure Land thought has been influenced by Christian ideas (by the Christian Nestorian sect of Ch'ang-an in east-central China, for example).

Origins of the Western Pure Land Concept

There are numerous theories regarding the origin of the Western Pure Land concept, Sukhāvatī. Some scholars look to an Indian derivation, others to an Iranian one, and still others to Judaic antecedents.

The latter has been proposed by Y. Iwamoto, who says that Sukhāvatī derives from the Garden of Eden. "'Eden,'" he writes, "is the Aramaic form of a Hebrew word that means 'pleasure.' Both Hebrew and Aramaic are western Semitic languages. The Old Testament was first compiled in Aramaic."[4] The Aramaic language and script were used by the Persian Achaemenid dynasty (7th–4th century B.C.E.), whose lands met India on the eastern border. The Indian script called Kharoṣṭhī developed under the influence of the Aramaic alphabet, and

Achaemenid architecture also affected India. There are thus sufficient grounds for believing that the name and concept of Eden could have entered India around this time.

Furthermore, the Judaic Eden and the Buddhist Sukhāvatī have many points in common. "Both are based on an idea of a particular direction, and both symbolize an oasis in a desert."[5] Eden is said to be in the east and Sukhāvatī in the west; moreover, *Eden* is derived from the Assyrian *edinnu* ("desert, plain"), and Sukhāvatī is an elaboration of Lake Anavatapta, itself a mythicized oasis. "As the Chinese translation of Anavatapta, 'no heat or fever,' indicates, it is clearly a mythicized desert oasis. The banks of the lake are adorned with gold, silver, lapis lazuli, and crystal; there is an abundance of gold sand; and the waves on the lake sparkle clear as a mirror, their waters pure and cold. It is very likely that the Sukhāvatī in the *Larger Sukhāvatī-vyūha* [Sūtra of Infinite Life] is an extension and enlargement of the legend of Lake Anavatapta and an exaggeration of its depiction."[6]

In Buddhist Sukhāvatī thought, the idea of the west is extremely important. If we look for the origin of Sukhāvatī in the Garden of Eden, how do we resolve such Biblical expressions as "God planted a garden eastward in Eden," "God placed at the east of the garden of Eden, Cher'u-bims, and a flaming sword that turned every way, to keep the way of the tree of life," and "the land of Nod, on the east of Eden," which offer no concept of the west? The Judaic ("eastward in Eden") and Buddhist paradises are even in opposite directions. Furthermore, the Buddhist concept of Sukhāvatī is connected with death; like the Egyptian Amnt and the Greek Elysion, it is the place to which the dead proceed. The Garden of Eden, however, is the earthly paradise from which Adam and Eve were expelled, and has no direct connection with death. In Christianity, the good go to Heaven, not to Eden. It seems we must look elsewhere for Sukhāvatī's origins.

I prefer to believe that Sukhāvatī has links with the Greek Elysion and the Egyptian Amnt. The Elysion of Greek mythology was also located in the west. In this mythology, some characteristic descriptions express the west in terms reminiscent of Sukhāvatī; for example, snow does not fall, there is no torrential rain, gentle breezes blow, trees bear golden fruit, and the Hesperides always dance. Homer described Elysion as a happy land ruled by the judge Rhadamanthus: "The immortals will send you to the Elysian Fields at the world's end, to join auburn-haired Rhadamanthus in the land where living is made easy for mankind, where no snow falls, no strong winds blow and there is never any rain, but day after day the West Wind's tuneful breeze comes in from the Ocean to refresh its people."[7] Later, Strabo, the Greek geographer and historian (64 B.C.E.–ca. 21 C.E.), commented that the "West Wind's tuneful breeze com[ing] in from the Ocean" indicates that Elysion is not only in the west, but also that it is a warm place.

Similar to the Elysian fields are the mythical Islands of the Blessed and the Garden of the Hesperides. The Islands of the Blessed are a place of happiness where the spring breezes blow and the trees bear golden flowers. Likewise, the Garden of the Hesperides is in the west, where the sun sets, near the edge of the ocean, and on its trees are golden fruits, guarded by the daughters of Hesperus, the Hesperides, whose pleasure is dancing and singing. According to Shigeichi Kure, as time passed poets such as Pindar (522?–442? B.C.E.) added an ethical element to the qualifications for rebirth in the Islands of the Blessed, describing them as a place where those who were virtuous in life enjoyed ease and happiness.[8]

M. P. Nilsson believes that the idea of Elysion came to Greece from Egypt by way of Crete.[9] From ancient times in Egypt, the idea prevailed that a person would be reborn after death in Amnt (the west), a land where there is no death, a place of happiness and joy, where a gentle breeze constantly blows. We find the following inscription at the grave of Harmhabi (a king of the 14th century B.C.E.): "On the left and on the right three large sailing ships are in a row and tow a gondola in which sit Harmhabi and his wife. This is the route of peace, leading toward Abydos, leading toward Osiris, the Good Being. The great lord is with you. In the west, in the west, the land of those who are good. The place that you loved cries in lamentation. Those who are drawing you on have achieved happiness. Your people embrace you. You, who proceed safely among those beloved by the lord, and against whom no wrong is found. Oh, Osiris Khent-amenti, permit a gentle breeze to blow upon him, permit him to join those who pay homage in the land of the living, Osiris Harmhabi!"[10]

Osiris is a god who died and lived again. A person who dies becomes Osiris and lives again in the land of the west, the name of which the Greek historian Plutarch (46?–120? C.E.) transmitted as *Amenthēs,* and which became *Amnt* in Coptic. This means that the ancient idea of Amnt still existed in the second century. There is also a strong possibility that the Osiris cult influenced the tradition of Jesus Christ's resurrection. If this is so, the Osiris cult still had considerable effect in the first and second centuries, though the rise of Christianity eventually annihilated it.

Ptolemy I (304–282 B.C.E.), ruler of Egypt, syncretized Greek and Egyptian religion in the invention of Sarapis. This deity was a fusion of the Greek Zeus (later the Roman Jupiter) and the Egyptian Osiris and Apis. He formed a trinity with Isis (an Egyptian goddess) and Harpocrates (Horus the Child). In the second century C.E., Egypt possessed forty-two temples to Sarapis, that in Alexandria being the most important. In 390 the Roman emperor Theodosius the Great, under whom Christianity became the official religion of the empire, destroyed the great image of Jupiter-Serapis in Alexandria.

How did Greek and Egyptian ideas of a western paradise find their way to India? From the second century B.C.E. to the second century C.E., under the Pax Romana, commercial and cultural exchange flourished between India and the Roman world. Iranian nomads (including the Kuṣāṇa dynasty, discussed below), invaded India and influenced culture there. This was truly an epoch of syncretism, and a time when many new religions became popular in India.

Evidence of this process can be found at Begrām, north of

Kabul in Afghanistan, the site of the ancient city of Kāpiśī. Hsüan-tsang visited it in the seventh century C.E. and wrote about it in his travel record. He noted that it had been the summer capital of Indian kings long ago, probably those of the Kuṣāṇa dynasty, who ruled from the first to the fourth century. It was during the middle of this period that the most famous of its kings, Kaniṣka, ruled. He is known in Buddhist literature as a patron of Buddhism.

The Kuṣāṇa dynasty originated in Central Asia. Their civilization was not urban, and they borrowed from more sophisticated neighboring cultures, including the Indian, Iranian, Greco-Roman, and Chinese (Han dynasty). Their coins document this with a variety of kingly titles: *rājātirāja* ("king of kings"), *mahārāja* ("great king"), and *devaputra* ("son of heaven"). These are, respectively, Iranian-, Indian-, and Chinese-derived titles. According to the French scholar André Maricq, however, *devaputra* is an Iranian-derived title.[11]

Kaniṣka II, a descendant of the first Kaniṣka, also adopted the title *kaisara,* derived from the Roman *caesar.* There is some doubt as to whether the term *basileus* ("king" in Greek) also existed. The Bactrian Greek rulers (in what is now northern Afghanistan) and their successors, the Śakas and Parthians, had formerly used it on coins. At the time of the Kuṣāṇas, who followed the Śakas and Parthians, the Greek usage may have been abandoned, but it is beyond doubt that the Kuṣāṇas, like their predecessors, were strong philhellenes. (It is of interest that the Parthian kings in Iran actually used "philhellene" as a name.)

There is also substantial material evidence for Greek and Egyptian influence in this Central Asian region. At the beginning of this century, French scholars unearthed many items of Greek and Egyptian origin from Begrām (ancient Kāpiśī), the probable site of the Kuṣāṇa capital. Many of these appeared to have originated in Alexandria and consisted largely of plaster and bronze statues of Greek gods and youths. Among the statues of gods were those of Silenus, satyrs, Eros, Psyche, Dionysus, maenads, Athena, and Hercules. Also found were a statue of the hero Odysseus (Ulysses) and an unusual form of a god, Serapis-Hercules. Indian goods are represented by an eye-catching openwork panel of ivory. Chinese lacquer was also found. The excavated items make it clear that a great deal of Greek culture had been imported from Alexandria.

We should mark in particular the statue of Serapis-Hercules in relation to the origin of the idea of a Western Pure Land of happiness. The American archaeologist B. Rowland, Jr. remarked on the syncretism of the statue, which was associated with the mystery religions: "This esoteric figure is immediately recognizable as a combination of Serapis and Hercules by the crown or modius ornamented with olive leaves as a symbol of the Nile's abundance and Hercules' familiar attributes of the club and the golden apples of the Hesperides."[12] Rowland has also identified another small statue excavated at Kāpiśī as the Egyptian god Harpocrates and the female figure on a glass cup as the goddess Isis. A statue of Harpocrates has also been excavated from Taxila in Pakistan. These discoveries indicate that the Alexandrine Serapis cult extended as far as the borders of India. An examination of the dates of the Buddhist sūtras in question seems to support these facts. The *Larger Sukhāvatī-vyūha* (1st century C.E.) was translated into Chinese at least five times between the years 148 and 258, a period corresponding to the middle Kuṣāṇa period, by translators from Parthia, the Kuṣāṇa empire, Samarkand (in Uzbekistan), and Kucha (in northwestern China). This supports the theory that Buddhist, Greek, and Egyptian religious ideas all flourished simultaneously in this region, with opportunities for mutual influence.

6. Buddhist Deities

Because its philosophy and practice are so difficult, Buddhism began as an elite religion. But Mahāyāna Buddhism did not forget the masses, and offered them an easier road to salvation: praying to buddhas, bodhisattvas, and gods.

Though Buddhism adopted large numbers of deities from other religions, it is essentially atheistic. The German philosopher Friedrich Nietzsche (1844–1900) praised Buddhism as a religion that had done away with the concept of God. Buddhist deities do not by any means represent the highest existence; they are thought of as standing below the Buddha, protecting the Buddha and the Dharma. Gods are above the realm of human beings, but the buddha-realm is above all existences, and it is human beings, not the gods, that are able to reach this state. It is not easy, for it takes enormous amounts of religious training, but theoretically human beings are able to surpass the gods.

Devas

We saw in chapter 2 that most Buddhist deities were adopted from Hinduism. Examples include the Four Great Kings, fairly low-ranking gods who guard the four sides of Mount Sumeru, and the thirty-three gods dwelling on the peak of that mountain.

The most important god of the latter group is Indra, a valiant warrior deity who was in ancient times the most popular of all the Indian gods. The Aryans worshiped Indra when they invaded India in about 1,500 B.C.E. and proceeded to conquer the indigenous population. When Indra was brought into Buddhism, though, his status was much reduced and he became merely a protector of the Buddha. This Indra is often called the heavenly lord Śakra (Śakro devānām indraḥ), which was translated into Chinese and Japanese as the compound *ten-taishaku,* literally, the "powerful one" (*shaku*) that is "lord" (*tai*) of the "gods" (*ten*).

Indra's origin appears to be linked with the Roman deity Jupiter. In ancient India people prayed to Indra for rain, believing he would smite the evil *nāgas* (serpents) that prevented rain from falling. Indra is a personification of lightning, and his weapon is the *vajra,* a thunderbolt. *Vajra* was translated into Chinese as a compound that means "diamond pounder." It is depicted in sculpture as an extremely simple weapon. A relief from northwestern India shows Śākyamuni attended by a god carrying this weapon, who is called either Vajra-pāṇi or Vajradhara, both forms meaning "*vajra*-wielding god." This god is a form of Indra, protector of the Buddha.

Dwelling in the sky above Indra is Yama, who later became the feared lord of the underworld. Above Yama's abode is the Tuṣita heaven, from which Śākyamuni was believed to have descended when he was born in India. It is now the dwelling place of the bodhisattva Maitreya, the future buddha who is now waiting to appear, examining the state of our world. There are many Yama and Tuṣita deities living with their wives and children. The deities in yet higher heavens, the Nirmāṇa-rati and Para-nirmita-vaśavartins, are comparatively senior gods, who find satisfaction in fulfilling their meager desires.

All of the deities mentioned so far belong to the realm of desire and are superior to human beings only in their greater strength, not because they are any less captive to desires. Above the realm of desire is that of form, from the lowest Brahmā heaven to the uppermost Akaniṣṭha heaven, each with its gods. Above that is the realm of formlessness, with its four heavens.

BUDDHAS

Though we have translated *deva* as "god" and "deity," there is a vast difference between the Indian gods and the modern Judeo-Christian idea of a deity. The Buddhist being that is closest to the Judeo-Christian notion of God is the Buddha. We cannot, though, in the narrowest sense of the word, call the Buddha a god.

In Judaism and Christianity, it was God who created the universe, and he exists in contradistinction to his creatures. In Mahāyāna Buddhism, the Buddha is the universe itself, and there is no distinction at all between the universe and the Buddha. Whereas Judaism and Christianity are monotheistic, Buddhism is pantheistic; that is, everything is god. The deity is everywhere—in each of us, in the smallest particle of dust, in the farthest corner of the universe. This idea was expressed in China by the phrase "plants and earth may all attain buddhahood." A pantheistic god is an unlikely object of faith, and there is even the possibility that pantheism may, at one end of its spectrum, verge into atheism (though pantheism allows religious emotion and atheism proceeds rationally, without regard for human sentiment).

At first, *the Buddha* meant Śākyamuni alone. Even today that remains true in countries that follow the Theravāda (a type of pre-Mahāyāna) tradition. At a very early period in Buddhist history, however, there arose the idea of the seven buddhas of the past: Vipassin (in Pali; Vipaśyin in Sanskrit), Sikhin (Śikhin), Vessabhū (Viśvabhū), Kakusandha (Krakucchanda), Koṇāgamana (Kanakamuni), Kassapa (Kāśyapa), and Sākyamuni (Śākyamuni). It is interesting to note that though Śākyamuni is the most recent of the buddhas, he is still considered a buddha of the past. As Mahāyāna developed, the buddhas of the past grew in number. In the *Larger Sukhāvatī-vyūha* (ca. 100 C.E.), eighty buddhas are said to have made their appearance while Amitābha Buddha was still training (the Chinese translation puts this number at fifty-three). The names of the seven buddhas of the past do not appear in this sūtra, perhaps indicating that the eighty buddhas belong to an even earlier period.

If we can conceive of buddhas of the past, we can also consider buddhas of the future, the most important of which is Maitreya, who will appear in this world 5,670,000,000 years after Śākyamuni's death. He is known as the "Future Savior," and some scholars think that this belief exhibits the influence of Messianic thought, which flourished in western Asia, including Iran, in the first and second centuries C.E.

As time went by, the numbers of buddhas thought to exist increased, and one thousand buddhas were described as inhabiting each *Kalpa* of Adornment of the past, each Auspicious *Kalpa* of the present, and each *Kalpa* of the Constellations of the future. The *Sūtra of the Auspicious Kalpa* (Bhadrakalpika-sūtra, trans. into Chinese ca. 300 C.E.) lists the names of the thousand buddhas of the Auspicious *Kalpa,* starting with Krakucchanda, Kanakamuni, Kāśyapa, Śākyamuni, and Maitreya. Only four of those listed were said to have appeared in the past, however.

At this moment, we live in the time between Śākyamuni's death and the coming of Maitreya. It thus seems correct to say that there is no buddha at present, although there are one thousand buddhas of the present *kalpa.* The idea of buddhas of the present may have grown out of a feeling of lack among some followers of Buddhism when they learned of the divinities of other religions, such as Ahura Mazda of Zoroastrianism and Jehovah of Judaism and Christianity. Amitābha, described in the next section, is such a buddha.

THREE BODIES DOCTRINE

The profusion of buddhas, including those like Bhaiṣajya guru (the Buddha of Healing) and Mahāvairocana, made some kind of systematization necessary. What emerged (ca. 2d or 3d century C.E.) was the "three bodies" (*tri-kāya*) theory, which describes the Buddha as having three bodies: the body of manifestation (*nirmāṇa-kāya*), the reward body (*saṃbhoga-kāya*), and the absolute, or Law, body (*dharma-kāya*).

The Law body is the Buddha as Truth itself, the fundamental buddha beyond shape or form, purely abstract. The Law body is the source of other bodies; it takes form in the manifestation and reward bodies. Mahāvairocana is the Law body. Followers of the Japanese Shingon sect, though they recognize many different buddhas, understand Mahāvairocana to be the supreme existence and venerate this buddha.

The body of manifestation, also called the transformation body, is the Buddha in human form. Pre-Mahāyāna Buddhism does not accept that Śākyamuni was anything but human, only that his abilities were vastly superior to those of an ordinary person. In Mahāyāna Buddhism however, Śākyamuni, the Buddha as Truth, is believed to have manifested himself in human form, and as such is termed "body of manifestation."

A good example of the reward body is Amitābha. Unlike Śākyamuni, this buddha is not a historical person, but a manifestation of the Law body. Amitābha appears in only some sūtras, and made a number of vows to save living beings (including one that promised salvation to any person who called his name). He practiced as a bodhisattva in life after life until he eventually attained buddhahood. Such a buddha is called a "reward body" because his body results from eons of religious practice. Those unable to gain enlightenment through their own efforts call upon Amitābha with all their might. Another example of the reward body is Bhaiṣajya-guru, the Buddha of Healing, who also made vows and has his own pure land. His statues are distinguished by the fact that they carry a medicine pot (perhaps originally the *maṇi* gem) in the left hand.

BODHISATTVAS

Bodhisattvas are beings undergoing religious training to attain buddhahood not only for themselves but also for other people; it is hard to say whether we should call them human beings or gods. Before becoming a buddha, Śākyamuni spent many existences as a bodhisattva, sometimes as a prince, sometimes as an elephant or a deer, but at all times manifesting his spirit of sacrifice and compassion. He trained in this way for three *asaṃkhya kalpas*. Many *Jātakas* relate the stories of his former lives.

Avalokiteśvara. One of the most famous bodhisattvas is Avalokiteśvara (Kuan-yin in Chinese; Kannon in Japanese). There are many theories about the meaning of this name. It was translated into Chinese using characters meaning "sound observer," that is, one who listens to sounds, or more specifically, to the cries of the suffering in the world. A second translation, Kuan-tzu-tsai, means "one who sees everything without hindrance." In the *Heart Sūtra* (Prajñāpāramitā-hṛdaya-sūtra, ca. 5th–6th century C.E.), Avalokiteśvara looks down on the world from on high, equipped with many powers and abilities.

The bodhisattva Avalokiteśvara appears not only in the Pure Land sūtras but also in the famous *Lotus Sūtra* (Saddharma-puṇḍarīka-sūtra, ca. 1st century C.E.). He is popular throughout Buddhist Asia and is strongly associated with the geographical spread of Mahāyāna Buddhism. The sculptures in Cave 90 at Kanheri, north of Bombay, depict Avalokiteśvara protecting devotees from shipwreck and wild beasts. The Chinese priest Fa-hsien (340?–420? C.E.) himself was shipwrecked twice on his return journey to China and called on Avalokiteśvara for deliverance from danger. Avalokiteśvara also came to be thought of as having his own Pure Land, called Potalaka. Local versions of this name are to be found in many places in China, Korea, and Japan. For example, Mount Futara (also called Nikkō) in Tochigi Prefecture, Japan, is a form of Potalaka, and in Lhasa, Tibet, the palace of the Dalai Lama is called Potala.

Statues of this bodhisattva are of many kinds. The usual form, the Holy Avalokiteśvara, is human in appearance. Another form is the Eleven-headed Avalokiteśvara, with ten small heads like a crown on top of an ordinary head, perhaps representing the various characteristics of the bodhisattva or symbolizing the bodhisattva's ability to see all those who are suffering in the world below. The Unfailing Fishing Line Avalokiteśvara carries a rope (*pāśa*) looped in his hand; this he casts to capture those who are evil and to pull in those who are suffering. In this he is unfailing (*amogha*). The Thousand-armed form expresses the idea that Avalokiteśvara saves numerous suffering beings. Paintings excavated in Central Asia show one thousand arms, as does a wooden statue at Tōshōdai-ji in Nara. Due to the difficulty of carving, statues having forty arms are more common, each arm being said to represent twenty-five abilities. The Thousand-eyed form is a similar concept and symbolizes the bodhisattva's encompassing power of salvation; the eyes are depicted on the palms of the hands. The Horse-headed Avalokiteśvara appears in sculpture as a human body and head with a horse's head on top. The origin and meaning of this form is not clear.

All these depictions are male, but female depictions also exist, such as the Kuan-yin called the wife of Ma-lang and the Cuṇḍī Avalokiteśvara. Ma-lang was a man whom Kuan-yin wanted to bring to the Buddhist faith. The bodhisattva therefore took the form of a woman, promising Ma-lang that she would marry him if he became a Buddhist. Because Avalokiteśvara expresses compassion, there was a strong tendency to link the image of the bodhisattva with that of a woman rather than a man. Moreover, in the Near East there existed a religion of the mother goddess, and Buddhists wanted a deity with the same characteristics. The Indic word *Avalokiteśvara* is a masculine noun, however, and people in India and Central Asia felt a certain reluctance to depict him in female form in sculpture; indeed, Avalokiteśvara always wears a mustache in that part of the world.

In China and Japan there is no grammatical gender, so people did not feel the same resistance to portraying the bodhisattva as female. Gradually the feminine form grew more and more prevalent. In Japan, most people think of Kannon as being a woman, and yearn for her loving warmth. A work by the nineteenth-century Japanese painter Kanō Hōgai, entitled *Compassionate Mother Kannon,* shows Kannon appearing above the clouds holding a staff in one hand, from the end of which dangles a thread. On the tip of this thread is a balloon-like object containing a baby. As the title indicates, the painting can be interpreted as a depiction of womanhood, and Kannon does have a woman's form. Nevertheless if we look closely at the face we can see a mustache, which recalls the Indian and Central Asian traditions.

Maitreya. Second only to Avalokiteśvara in popularity is Maitreya, whose name derives from *maitrī,* meaning "benevolence." His cult grew at about the same time as that of Avalokiteśvara and perhaps even predates it. He is the Future Buddha, who now resides in the Tuṣita heaven. Later there arose the belief that it was relatively easy to reach the Tuṣita heaven and that even an ordinary person might hope to achieve the religious training necessary to go there. This supported the cult of those who sought rebirth in that heaven. Between the third and seventh centuries the cult was extremely popular in eastern Asia. Early in the fifth century, the Chinese priest Fa-hsien crossed the Pamirs on the way from China to India. Deep in the Karakoram Range he came across a large wooden statue of Maitreya. The local people told him that Buddhism had begun spreading outside India when the statue was erected. After Śākyamuni's death it was therefore Maitreya who had the ability to spread Buddhist teachings. The Maitreya faith subsequently gained great popularity in China, and spread from there to the Korean Peninsula and Japan. Among the statues in the Hōryū-ji Treasure House at the Tokyo National Museum, there are many figures of Miroku (Maitreya), depicted sitting with one leg resting on the other knee and the right hand raised, touching the chin. Around the eighth century, the Maitreya cult's popularity waned, perhaps because of the rise of the Avalokiteśvara cult.

Bodhisattvas and Pure Land thought. Also competing with the Maitreya cult was that of Amitābha Buddha (Amida in Japanese). His statues are often shown accompanied by two attendants, Avalokiteśvara and Mahāsthāmaprāpta. With the rise of Pure Land thought, people began to ask which cult, that of Amitābha or Maitreya, was the most effective for salvation, and to wonder if it would be better to be reborn in the Pure Land of Sukhāvatī or in the Tuṣita heaven. It was, in fact, a straightforward decision: whereas the Tuṣita heaven was merely one of many abodes in the realm of desire, with its lord not a buddha but a bodhisattva, the Pure Land of Sukhāvatī was a buddha-land where the defilements no longer existed, and its lord was a buddha. No doubt proponents of the Pure Land cult would have stressed that a place like the Tuṣita heaven was neither one thing nor the other; rebirth there did not preclude falling at some later time into the lower realms. In eastern Asia, the Maitreya cult gradually weakened, while that of Amitābha grew ever more popular.

Other bodhisattvas. Mañjuśrī, the bodhisattva of wisdom, is depicted riding on a lion. Samantabhadra symbolizes Buddhist meditation and is shown riding an elephant. Though Brahmā and Indra appear in early pre-Mahāyāna Buddhist carvings, Mañjuśrī and Samantabhadra belong only to the later Mahāyāna tradition. Kṣitigarbha is determined to deliver all the beings of the world from their suffering. Like Amitābha Buddha, he has undergone eons of religious training, but Kṣitigarbha has appeared in this world without accepting buddhahood. He is usually depicted as a bodhisattva with a shaved head. Other bodhisattvas portrayed frequently in Buddhist art include Sūryaprabha ("sunlight") and Candraprabha ("moonlight"), the attendants of Bhaiṣajya-guru; and Mahāsthāmaprāpta, who symbolizes wisdom and is one of the attendants of Amitābha.

Because bodhisattvas are still undergoing religious training, living beings of this world may be called bodhisattvas. Asaṅga and Vasubandhu, great Buddhist philosophers of the fifth century, have been given the title of bodhisattva, as have Gyōgi (668–749) and Nichiren (1222–82) in Japan.

Avatars. The idea of the temporary transformation (*gonge* or *gongen* in Japanese) of buddhas and bodhisattvas is a distinctive feature of Buddhism. For example, the universal Buddha Mahāvairocana manifests himself in the form of Śākyamuni or Maitreya, and Avalokiteśvara may appear in the eleven-headed form or in the form of Ma-lang's wife, adopting whichever manifestation best suits the circumstances.

This idea appeared in Buddhism after the rise of Mahāyāna; it derives from the Hindu concept of avatars, or incarnations. Viṣṇu, one of Hinduism's chief deities, has ten incarnations, including a boar, a lion, and the Buddha. Because followers of Hinduism consider Śākyamuni to be an avatar of Viṣṇu, they tend to view Buddhism as part of their own religion. The idea of avatars has been extremely effective in the spread of Buddhism from region to region, allowing Buddhism to absorb the gods of other countries as temporary manifestations of its own deities. The Japanese *kami* (nature gods and deified heroes) were thus declared to be avatars of particular Indian deities. For example, Hachiman, said to be the deified emperor Ōjin, was identified as a great bodhisattva, a Buddhist avatar.

Female Deities

As in the Orient, many female deities were worshiped in India in the common era. Many Hindu male deities (*devas*) have a wife (*devī*) or wives, who are naturally viewed as goddesses. In this period, female deities became more popular than before, because people saw them as symbols of abundance and tenderness.

Lakṣmī, the consort of Viṣṇu, was adopted by Buddhists as their most authentic female deity. She is a favorite subject in art; particularly famous are a painting at Yakushi-ji and a statue at Jōruri-ji, both in Nara. Lakṣmī personifies beauty and, like Aphrodite (Venus), rose from the waves. Her son Kāma, like

Eros (Cupid), is the god of love. Both Kāma and Eros pierce human hearts with an arrow. So close are the parallels between the Greek and Hindu myths that one is led to believe that there must have been some direct western influence.

In Vedic times (1,000–500 B.C.E.), Sarasvatī was a river personified by a goddess. The area of Pakistan in which five rivers flow is called the Punjab, which literally means "five rivers." In ancient times, though, the region had a name meaning "seven rivers." Sarasvatī was one of the two rivers that dried up due to climatic changes. Later Sarasvatī became the goddess of eloquence, wisdom, and music. In Japan she has become part of folk belief and is counted as one of the seven gods of fortune (the Chinese character for the *zai* component of her name in translation is expressed as "wealth" rather than "learning"). Her shrines, like the one at Enoshima in Japan, still tend to be found near water, befitting her origin as a river deity.

Hārītī is invoked today for the health of children and for an easy birth. In India she was originally a demon who fed on small children. Legend says that grieving villagers appealed to the Buddha to deliver them from her, and so the Buddha hid one of her ten thousand children from her. Mad with grief, Hārītī searched frantically for the missing child and then, unable to find it, went to the Buddha for help, believing him omniscient. "Here you are," said the Buddha, "grief-stricken because one of your ten thousand children is missing. How do you think the villagers, who have only two or three, feel when they lose one?" Hārītī then awoke to the extent of her wrongdoing and became a deity that protected children.

Carvings found in the Punjab depict Hārītī with a kind face, seated on a chair surrounded by five or six children and holding another to her breast, with other children in her lap, or surrounded by children playing at her feet. Many statues show her holding a pomegranate, a many-seeded fruit that symbolizes fertility. Pomegranates are grown widely in the dry heartland of Pakistan and Afghanistan, which suggests that the Hārītī cult originated somewhere in northwestern India.

Another female deity that should be mentioned is Marīci, literally "mirage," a goddess who entered Buddhism from Hinduism. She rides before the sun, and is a personification of the sun's rays. She also personifies the "wave of vapor," that is, a wave of heated air on a summer street. Perhaps because of this, in Japan she became the protector-goddess of samurai, who wanted to conceal themselves like transparent vapor.

MAHĀKĀLA

Before we leave the Indian deities I would like to touch upon Mahākāla, the "great black one." I-ching, a Chinese priest who visited India in the seventh century, commented that a wooden statue of the "great black deity" (Daikoku-ten in Japanese) stood beside the dining pillar in the temples, that it was continually blackened with oil, and that the deity had a protective function. From early times in Japan Mahākāla was revered as a deity of good luck, apparently confused with an ancient native *kami* called Ōkuninushi no mikoto. (This confusion doubtless arose because both names can be pronounced "daikoku," according to alternative readings of the Chinese characters.) It became the custom to call the central pillar of the house the *daikoku-bashira* (*hashira,* "pillar"). I think, despite the different explanations that appear in Japanese dictionaries, that this expression derived from the pillar upon which Daikoku-ten was venerated.

Why this god is black we do not know. It may be significant that Marco Polo, writing in the thirteenth century, remarked that in southern India black was revered and white despised.[1] When the Aryans entered the Indian subcontinent, they made a distinction between themselves, whom they thought of as white, and the aboriginal inhabitants, whom they considered black. The Hindi term *varṇa,* meaning "color," is the common Indian term for the system of four castes that divides society, and so it may be thought that the caste system is the result of white supremacy. By the time Marco Polo arrived in southern India, however, it appears that the old way of thinking had been turned about, and black had come to be thought superior. The name of Kṛṣṇa, the best known of Hindu deities, means "black," as does that of the grim goddess Kālī, "the black one." Perhaps Mahākāla shares the same tradition.

Demigods

Protectors of Buddhism. There are a large number of demigods in Buddhism, which could be defined as either demons or gods, for they share characteristics of both. The demigods have traditionally been grouped into eight kinds of beings that protect Buddhism: *devas, nāgas, yakṣas, gandharvas, asuras, garuḍas, kiṃnaras,* and *mahoragas.* Carvings of these can be seen, for example, at Kōfuku-ji in Nara, Japan.

We have dealt already with *devas;* they are of course not demigods but gods.

The *nāga* is a personified snake, in particular the cobra, the object of a widespread cult in India. Throughout the world the snake is linked with the bringing forth of water, perhaps because snakes are found near water or because their movements resemble a twisting river.

Yakṣas tend to be wild, demonic beings; they were originally tree deities and spirits of the villages and woodlands. Though they are thought of as frightful in aspect, female *yakṣas* are depicted in Indian sculpture as beautiful and erotic. In Japan they seem to have terribly cold hearts, lending meaning to the popular Japanese expression "the face of a bodhisattva and the heart of a *yakṣa.*" In China and Japan *yakṣas* were almost always shown as terrifying beings.

Gandharvas are Indra's retainers, and they are represented as celestial singers and musicians who feast on perfumes.

Asuras are the demonic enemies of the gods (*devas*). *Asura* shares the same derivation as *ahura* ("lord") of ancient Iran. Interestingly, Ahura Mazda, the supreme god of Zoroastrianism, means "radiant lord," whereas *daevas* in Persian means "violent and amoral destroyers."

In Hinduism, the *garuḍa* is a mythical bird, the personification of the eagle and the steed of Viṣṇu. Indian sculpture portrays the *garuḍa* as an eagle, but in Central Asia it is depicted as a human body with an eagle's wings, talons, and beak. In China and Japan the image of the *tengu* ("heavenly fox") accreted to that of the *garuḍa,* resulting in portrayals of a being with wings and a long nose, the latter perhaps a misrepresentation of a beak. It is also possible that the depiction of the *garuḍa* was influenced by the *gigaku* and *gagaku* masks of the Nara and Heian periods in Japan, which include representations of *karura* (*garuḍa*) and *suikoō* ("drunken barbarian kings") with large noses.

Kiṃnaras are a type of bird. The Sanskrit word means "Is it human?" revealing the half-human, half-bird nature of this being. It does not exhibit the *garuḍa*'s fearsome aspect but is gentle in appearance. The deity of music, the *kiṃnara* derives from the same source as the Greek goddess of the moon, Selene. In Japan this type of being is called a *karyōbinga* (*kalaviṅka* in Sanskrit).

The *mahoraga* ("boa") is a personification of a large snake.

Rākṣasas. Other demonic demigods include the *rākṣasas,* demons and devils connected with the island of Sri Lanka. In the *Rāmāyaṇa* (Romance of Rāma), one of India's two great epics, they appear as inhabitants of that island. A modified form of that legend entered Buddhism, relating that there lived in Sri Lanka five hundred female *rākṣasas,* who captured and ate shipwrecked merchants.[2] This perhaps hints at the existence somewhere in India of a tribe that ate human flesh. Herodotus mentions a tribe of Indians called the Callatiae (Kallatiai), who ate their parents' dead bodies, and another called the Padaei (Padaioi), who killed the sick in order to eat their meat before it was destroyed by illness.[3] This is a good example of the way some people are viewed as demons because of their different customs and manners.

Other demigods. Another monster is Kumbhāṇḍa, a demon with testicles as huge as a waterpot. So big are they, in fact, that he is able to use them as a seat, and he can only walk if he holds them up out of the way. I was inclined to think of this as pure fantasy until I saw some photographs of enlarged testicles caused by a parasite, a condition called elephantiasis. It is a disease prevalent in hot countries, including southern India. A colleague commented on the similarity of this aspect of Kumbhāṇḍa with the traditional ceramic depiction of the raccoon dog, the *tanuki,* as having enormous testicles. The Kumbhāṇḍa of India and the *tanuki* of Japan may both be fantastic representations of an actual condition.

Kumbhīra is the personification of the crocodile and thus is associated with water. He came to be regarded as a water deity, the protector of shipping. He is enshrined in Japan as Kompira and is familiarly known as Kompira-sama. Kompira's most famous shrine is found in Kagawa Prefecture on Shikoku. Since the Meiji period (1868–1912) this shrine has been formally called the more Shintō-sounding Kotohira Shrine, the result of government efforts to separate the closely entwined Buddhist and Shintō traditions.

Gods of the Esoteric Tradition

Esoteric Buddhism, the last stage in the religious development of Buddhism in India, appeared suddenly in India around the latter half of the seventh century C.E. One of its features is ultrasymbolism, in which minor differences in the position of the fingers symbolize one or another great truth. In the same way, single letters or syllables (*bīja,* "seed") symbolize particular deities. Another feature of esoteric Buddhism is affirmation of worldly desires. Early Buddhists endeavored to escape from the defiled world and the stained self. Esoteric Buddhism, however, declares that worldly desires are emancipation, perhaps because everything is a manifestation of the cosmic Buddha. Thus in this type of Buddhism appear deities who are possessed of anger, desire, passion, and other intense feelings. Furthermore, esoteric Buddhism grew under the enormous influence of Hinduism, with the result that virtually all the Hindu deities entered Buddhism at that time.

Acala. Acala is depicted surrounded by flames and has a fierce countenance. His mind is immovable (*acala*), and he consumes evil with his fire. Some paintings and statues of Acala show his body as red and others, yellow or blue. There thus arose a custom of referring to Acala in terms of color, such as the Red Acala or the Yellow Acala. Still other color designations are made in terms of the color of his eyes, such as the Black-eyed Acala or the White-eyed Acala.

Rāga Vidyārāja. Rāga means "red," and symbolizes the blood running hotly through a body overwhelmed by desires, and so has the connotation of being stained by the passions. Pre-Mahāyāna Buddhism taught people to cast away the passions and defilements and to seek enlightenment. Mahāyāna brought changes in this doctrine, and by the time esoteric Buddhism held sway, the defilements were considered to be in themselves enlightenment, which meant that this life of ours, full to bursting with defilements and passions, is itself the enlightened state. This idea came from Hindu tantrism.

Pre-Mahāyāna Buddhism, however, taught that a life stained by the passions is a life steeped in delusion, and that it therefore must be purified. It is Rāga Vidyārāja who performs that cleansing. He is generally portrayed with a red body, symbolizing both the defilements themselves and their purification. The epithet *vidyārāja,* shared also by Acala, belongs to those divinities who express enlightened wisdom through a passionate aspect.

Gaṇeśa. Gaṇeśa, with an elephant's head and a human body, often appears in the form of embracing male and female figures, an expression of enlightenment through the unity of male and female.

Mahāyāna Buddhism was influenced by the Hindu idea that the Absolute (Brahman, the universe or world essence) is identical with the Self (Ātman). To an enlightened person the two are one, for with enlightenment comes the loss of all egotistic consciousness. We usually consider the world and the self to be in opposition, the self working as the subject of action. Such an attitude is, however, a delusion. Those who wish to arrive at this truth must undergo various kinds of religious training. Some practitioners of Tantric (esoteric) Buddhism taught that the realm of true enlightenment could be reached through the unity of male and female. By means of the sexual act the practitioner could enter a state of rapture, losing all sense of self and so penetrating the truth of the oneness of Brahman and Ātman. Gaṇeśa symbolizes this idea.[4]

7. The Buddha and the Cosmos

As we have seen, pre-Mahāyāna Buddhism makes a distinction between the realm where the Buddha dwells and the realm of delusion. Although Mahāyāna Buddhism also posits the existence of buddha-realms and our own defiled world, another key element of Mahāyāna cosmology is the premise that the Buddha is omnipresent in our own realm. As this idea developed, the Buddha came to be equated with the world. The origin of this view is an attempt to interpret the nature of a buddha by positing the existence of various buddha bodies.

For followers of pre-Mahāyāna Buddhism, the Buddha was a historical figure; he had already entered nirvāṇa (eternal peace), so he did not now inhabit this world. The stūpa was none other than a grave, a construction symbolizing the Buddha's death.[1] As time and distance between the Buddha and his followers increased during the centuries following his death, believers tended to deify the Buddha. The *Lotus Sūtra* (1st century C.E.), which speaks of an eternal Buddha of whom the historical Buddha is no more than a single manifestation, and above all the *Flower Garland Sūtra* (Avataṃsaka-sūtra, ca. 3d–4th century C.E.), express the idea that numerous buddhas exist simultaneously in the universe. This is a fundamental principle of Mahāyāna Buddhism.

In a relief called "Miracle at Śrāvastī" (photo 5), Śākyamuni manifests himself as a multitude of buddhas in order to gain acceptance among followers of non-Buddhist sects. The miracle at

Śrāvastī is a pre-Mahāyāna theme, but the relief can also certainly be interpreted in terms of the *Flower Garland Sūtra.* It may even have been created to express that sūtra's teachings that the Buddha is present everywhere in the universe (note the lotus throne on which the Buddha sits, a Mahāyāna element). The *Heavenly Stories* (Divyāvadāna, 3d–4th century C.E.) describes the miracle at Śrāvastī as *buddhāvataṃsaka* ("adornment, or glorious manifestation, of the Buddha"). This expression is identical to that used in the full title of the *Flower Garland Sūtra,* Mahāvaipulya-buddhāvataṃsaka-sūtra. It means that countless buddhas manifest themselves in this realm, thereby adorning it. To understand this idea more fully, we must first explore the cosmology of the Lotus Repository World, which graphically pictures the Buddha's multiplicity and all-pervading presence.

It is important to keep in mind that the concepts of the Lotus Repository World and the pure lands have different origins. Furthermore, the pure lands are located outside Sahā (our world), while the Lotus Repository World embraces all worlds, including the *trichiliocosm,* the largest conception of space in pre-Mahāyāna Buddhism.

The Lotus Repository World

It is interesting that the Chinese translated *avataṃsaka* in the *Flower Garland Sūtra*'s title as *hua-yen,* literally, "flower adornment." Though the word *flower* (or *lotus*) does not appear in the Sanskrit title, it was incorporated into the Chinese because the sūtra describes the universe as a lotus flower. The chapter of the sūtra titled "Lotus Repository World" describes the universe in the following way.[2]

The universe contains layers upon layers of wind circles, as portrayed in figure 25, equivalent in number to the particles of sand there would be if Mount Sumeru were ground into dust. The lowest wind circle is called Abode of Equality. The surface of this wind circle is filled with jeweled ornamentation, shining as brightly as a flame. The wind circle above that is called

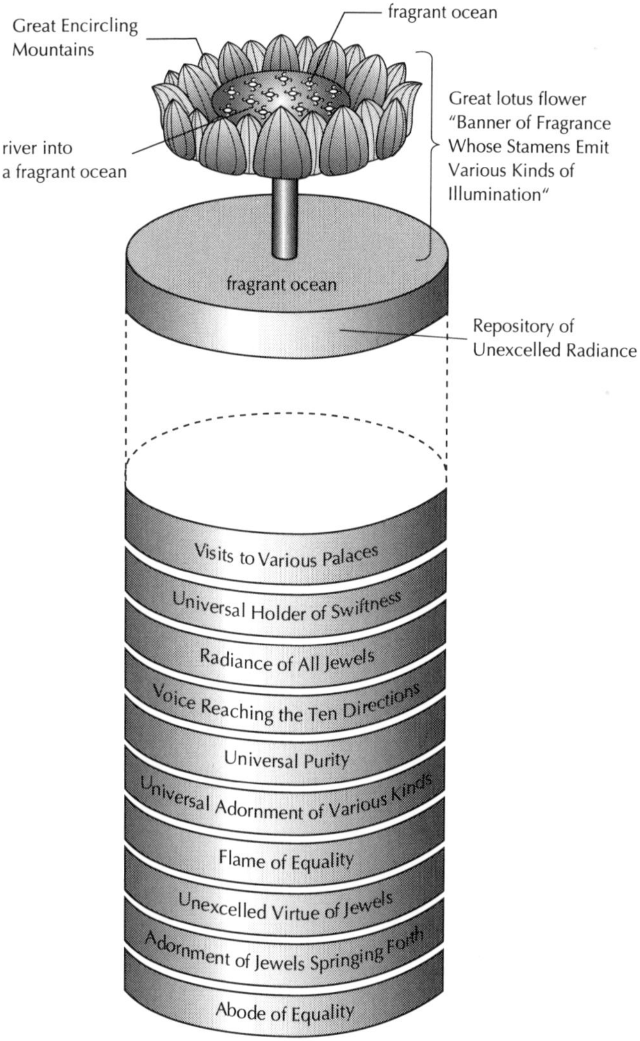

Fig. 25. Layers of Wind Circles and the Great Lotus Flower that Blooms on Them, according to the *Flower Garland Sūtra*

Adornment of Jewels Springing Forth; here banners adorned with that supreme jewel, the *maṇi,* are radiant with light. The sūtra describes the first ten lower layers in detail; the uppermost wind circle is called Repository of Unexcelled Radiance. Above that is a fragrant ocean, in which blooms a great lotus flower, called Banner of Fragrance Whose Stamens Emit Various Kinds of Illumination. Because it is easily understood, the actual lotus flower is used as an object of meditation, and the *Flower Garland Sūtra* enlarges and embellishes this flower in its description of the universe (see figure 26).

The fragrance comes from the closely packed stamens or, more accurately, from the anthers of the stamens, and lights shine within. This great lotus, standing like a banner in the center of the fragrant ocean, contains the Lotus Repository World. The petals of the lotus, standing in peaks, are its Great Encircling Mountains. The nectar in the center of the flower is the fragrant water, and the stamens are the jeweled trees and sweet-smelling grass.

The receptacle in the center of the great lotus is the land of the Lotus Repository World. Made of diamond, the land is hard, pure, and flat. Just as a lotus flower contains seeds, a number of holes in the receptacle contain the fruit. These are the "fragrant oceans" of the Lotus Repository World, as numerous as "the number of atoms in indescribably many buddha-fields."

Fig. 26. The Lotus Repository World as a Symbol of the Structure of the Universe

The floors of these oceans and their shores are made of jewels, and their translucent waters reflect the colors of the various jewels. Jeweled flowers surround them, and sandalwood powder settles on their floors. The Buddha's voice is heard, and bodhisattvas hold parasols. There are stairways and balustrades made of the ten jewels, and countless palaces, forests, and white lotuses. Into the fragrant oceans flow many fragrant rivers with jeweled banks circling the oceans to the right. The rivers emit jeweled clouds of the buddhas and the sounds of the speech of living beings. The actions and forms of the buddhas emerge from the swirling of the waters. The land between the rivers is also variously adorned.

The *Flower Garland Sūtra* goes on to say, "In these oceans of fragrant water, as numerous as the atoms in indescribably many buddha-fields, rest world systems as numerous as the atoms in indescribably many buddha-fields." I interpret this to mean that in one fragrant ocean there is one world system, so that the number of the oceans and the number of world systems is the same, rather than that there are indescribably large numbers of world systems in each ocean. I base my interpretation on the fact that a lotus flower has a single seed (actually, fruit) in each hole. I also believe that "system" (expressed by the character for "seed" in Chinese) is an expression derived from an actual lotus seed. The various world systems differ according to the ocean on which they rest; they are richly varied in both shape and substance.

The fragrant ocean in the middle of the great lotus is called Boundless Light of Wonderful Flowers, and the world system in this ocean is Blazing Jewel Light Illuminating the Ten Directions.[3] Twenty worlds exist along the vertical axis through the center of the world system, and each of these worlds is surrounded by countless worlds (see figure 27). This scheme is expressed on the pedestal of the Great Buddha Vairocana at Tōdai-ji temple in Nara, Japan. The lowest of these twenty worlds is called Omnipresent Illumination of Supreme Light; it is surrounded by worlds "as numerous as the atoms in one

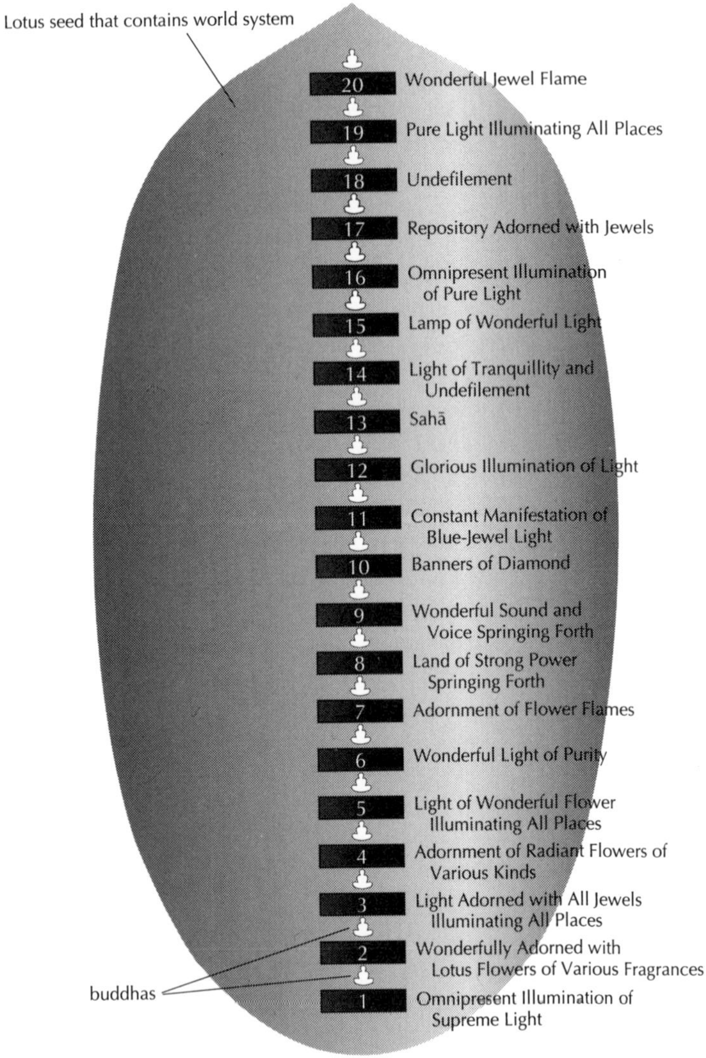

Fig. 27. The World System at the Center of the Lotus Repository World
Twenty worlds, each with its buddha, exist in a world system called Blazing Jewel Light Illuminating the Ten Directions; infinite worlds surround each of the twenty worlds, and the number of surrounding worlds increases as the sequence extends upward.

buddha-field." The buddha of this world is called Undefiled Lamp of the Eye of Purity. The next world above this is called Wonderful Adornment with Lotus Flowers of Various Fragrances, surrounded by worlds "as numerous as the atoms of two buddha-fields." The buddha of this world is called Supreme Leonine Illuminating Radiance. Eventually we come to the highest world, called Wonderful Jewel Flame, surrounded by worlds "as numerous as the atoms of twenty buddha-fields," whose buddha is called Radiance with Fortune and Virtue. It is of interest to note that the thirteenth world in the series is called Sahā. This is "our" world. The occupants of the other worlds are not specified, but we may assume that beings do inhabit them.

The great number of worlds in just one lotus seed exemplifies the reproductive power of a single seed. One lotus seed will give birth to a great lotus containing uncountable cells, and even while the lotus is still in formation, it probably holds within itself the existence of its own descendants, just as a human female fetus is thought already to possess many ova.

The possibility inherent within the seed had already been discussed in the Hindu *Upaniṣads* (ca. 600 B.C.E.) in a conversation between a philosopher and his son Śvetaketu Āruṇeya.

> "Bring me a fruit from that banyan tree."
> "Here it is, father."
> "Break it."
> "It is broken, father."
> "What do you see there?"
> "I see extremely tiny seeds, father."
> "Break one of them."
> "It is broken, father."
> "What do you see there?"
> "I can see nothing at all."
> And then the father said to his son, "My son, it is from the subtle essence within the seed that you cannot see that this great tree exists. My son, believe what I say. That infinitesimal

> subtle essence, which you cannot see, is the spirit of all the universe. It is this that is true. It is this that is Ātman. And you are it."[4]

It is said, incidentally, that a lotus seed retains its power of germination for a thousand years.

The Lotus Repository World contains even more world systems than those already discussed. East of the central fragrant ocean lies another ocean (see figure 28), called Repository of Undefiled Flames. Its world system is called Omnipresent Illumination of the Vortex of Fields, and contains twenty layers of worlds. The lowest of these twenty worlds, called Banner of Adornment of the Palace, is surrounded by world systems "as numerous as the atoms of one buddha-field" and has a buddha called Radiance Emitted from between Eyebrows Illuminating All Directions. The other worlds are similar to those of the world system examined earlier. A third ocean, south of the second, is called Ring of Inexhaustible Radiance; it supports a world system called

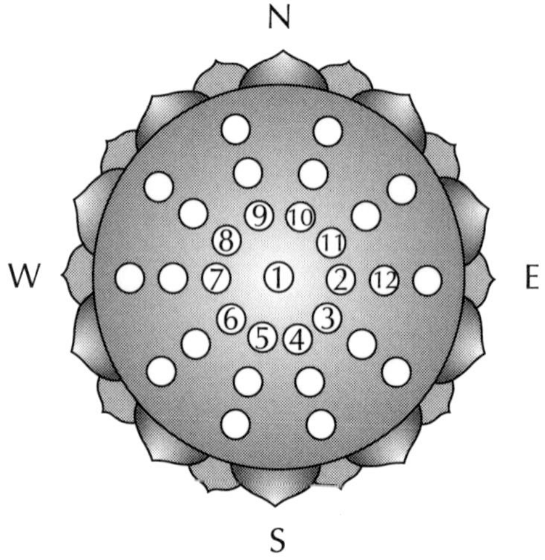

Fig. 28. Simplified Arrangement of Fragrant Oceans in the Lotus Repository World
1) Boundless Light of Wonderful Flowers, 2) Repository of Undefiled Flames, 3) Ring of Inexhaustible Radiance

Adorned with the Buddha's Banners. Though it, too, has twenty layers of worlds, the sūtra describes only nineteen, hinting at a possible copying error. To the right of this ocean there is a fourth, and so on to the eleventh. The twelfth is to the east of the second fragrant ocean (Repository of Undefiled Flames), and from the thirteenth to the twenty-first, the oceans are described as being "outward" from the seas numbered three to eleven (see figure 28). The sūtra says that there are as many fragrant oceans as the atoms in indescribably many buddha-fields, and that they extend beyond each other to the encircling mountains. It considerably abbreviates the details of the outer world systems, only generally describing the first, tenth, thirteenth, and twentieth.

The sūtra goes on to characterize oceans of worlds of other lotus worlds. To the east of the Lotus Repository World is the ocean of worlds called Adorned with Pure and Radiant Lotus Flowers, to the south is the ocean of worlds called Repository Adorned with the Radiance of All Jeweled Moons, and there are further oceans to the west, north, northeast, southeast, southwest, northwest, nadir, and zenith. In all of them are worlds, with their buddhas and countless bodhisattvas. The oceans of worlds, although finite in number, are not limited to these eleven but are "as numerous as the atoms of a myriad buddha-fields."

These countless oceans of worlds "undergo changes over *kalpas* as numerous as there are atoms in the oceans of worlds," as described in chapter 4. Far in the past, more than twice "the *kalpas* as numerous as the atoms of the worlds," there were oceans of worlds different from those of today.

VAIROCANA AND THE MULTIPLICITY OF BUDDHAS

The splendid Lotus Repository World was made by the buddha Vairocana, who undertook religious practice for *kalpas* as numerous as "there are atoms in the ocean of worlds." He associated in each *kalpa* with buddhas as numerous "as there are atoms in the ocean of worlds," and practiced in purity, in the presence of those buddhas, great vows as numerous "as there are atoms in the ocean of worlds." As a result of the power of those actions, the Lotus Repository World came into being.

The word *Vairocana* means "illuminating all places." The element *roc-* has the same derivation as the Latin *lux* ("light"). When Mahāyāna Buddhism was developing, cults of a sun deity spread throughout India, the Orient, and Europe. Vairocana was described as a solar deity and, around the seventh century C.E., developed into the esoteric buddha Mahāvairocana, who is the abstract, fundamental buddha beyond shape or form. The connection between a lotus flower and the sun is worth noting. Flowers open as the sun rises and close as it sets. Their petals are also reminiscent of the rays of light extending from the sun's disk. Incidentally, many paintings from ancient Egypt portray a solar deity being born from a lotus or, to be accurate, a water lily.

Various passages in the *Flower Garland Sūtra* describe how Vairocana Buddha penetrates and fills the cosmos:

> The vast fields that the Buddha has adorned are equal in number to all atoms. Pure children of the Buddha fill these lands and cause to fall the rain of the finest, mysterious dharma [teaching]. As we see the Buddha sitting at this assembly, we see the Buddha sitting in the same way in all atoms. The body of the Buddha neither departs nor comes but all the same is manifested clearly in all the realms (ch. 1).

> In every grain of dust of the Lotus Repository World can be seen the dharma-essence (ch. 5).

> The Tathāgata [the Buddha] manifests himself in all the lands of the ten directions, but his actual body is undifferentiated. It is like the full moon appearing in its entirety in dewdrops upon the ground (ch. 24).

The *Sūtra of the Perfect Net* (Brahmajāla-sūtra, ca. 3d century C.E.), a Mahāyāna Vinaya (precepts) text, presents a different depiction of a world resting upon a lotus, which nevertheless also shows the Buddha's multiplicity and omnipresence. Vairocana sits upon a great thousand-petaled lotus, each petal of which supports a world. He incarnates into one thousand Śākyamuni Buddhas, one for each of the worlds (see figure 29). On each petal, in each world, there are ten billion Mount Sumeru worlds. The Śākyamuni Buddhas each incarnate into ten billion

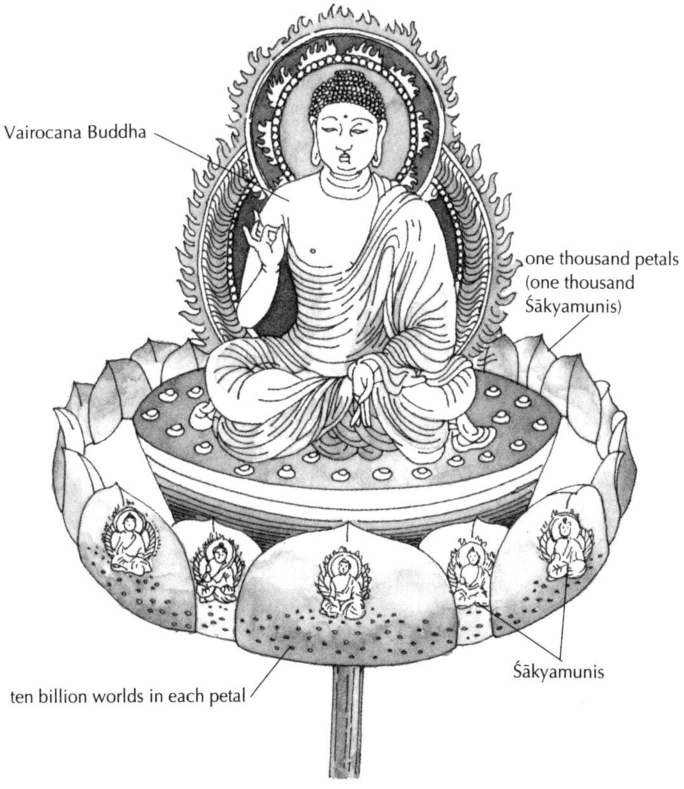

Fig. 29. Lotus Pedestal World according to the *Sūtra of the Perfect Net*

Śākyamuni Bodhisattvas, who dwell within each of these Mount Sumeru worlds. We therefore have a total of one Vairocana Buddha, one thousand Śākyamuni Buddhas, and ten trillion Śākyamuni Bodhisattvas.

Each lotus petal is more or less equivalent to one great-thousand-world. I say "more or less" because although the *Sūtra of the Perfect Net* mentions that there are ten billion worlds on each petal, the pre-Mahāyāna tradition defines a great-thousand-world as consisting of only one billion worlds. I should also point out similarities between Hindu myth and the *Sūtra of the Perfect Net*'s Lotus Pedestal World. In the Hindu tradition, Brahmā was brought forth by Viṣṇu from a thousand-petaled lotus growing from Viṣṇu's navel and, sitting on the lotus, he created the world.

The famous Great Buddha of Tōdai-ji in Nara, Japan (see photo 6), was modeled on the iconography of the *Sūtra of the Perfect Net.* The Great Buddha, who is of course Vairocana, sits on a lotus-shaped base, around which petals are carved. There should theoretically be one thousand petals, but this proved impossible to cast, so there are only a few dozen. On the upper part of each petal is engraved a Śākyamuni surrounded by bodhisattvas, with twenty-six horizontal lines (photos 7 and 8) beneath Śākyamuni that separate the buddha from several abstract Mount Sumeru worlds. Only one Mount Sumeru world appears in photo 8; of course it is impossible to depict ten billion of them on each petal. The twenty-six horizontal lines seem to represent the twenty-five realms above and including the Yama heaven (that is, the four heavens of the realm of desire, the seventeen heavens of the realm of form, and the four abodes of the realm of formlessness, as described in chapters 2 and 3).

The Cosmic Vairocana

A wall-painting from Khotan shows a buddha figure with the world depicted on his body (see photos 9 and 10). Joanna Williams has called this the Cosmic Vairocana.[5] The design on the buddha's chest suggests the Hindu legend of the Churning of the Ocean. In this legend, Viṣṇu, in his incarnation as a tortoise, dove to the bottom of the ocean, and allowed his back to serve as the base for Mount Mandara. This mountain became a churning rod, and the great serpent (*nāga*) Vāsuki, wrapped around the mountain, became a rope. With this the gods churned up the ocean and were thus able to recover objects lost in the great flood, including the nectar of immortality (*amṛta*). The Khotan wall-painting shows a two-headed snake (Vāsuki is one-headed). The scene depicted may or may not be related to the legend of the Churning of the Ocean, but it has a striking connection with the cosmos of the *Flower Garland Sūtra*. Śikṣānanda, this sūtra's translator, was born in Khotan, and some scholars believe the sūtra was composed there.

In the sixteenth-century novel *Monkey*, by Wu Ch'eng-en, there is a famous episode concerning an altercation between Monkey and the Buddha. "Jump off the palm of my right hand," challenged the Buddha, and stretched out his right hand, about the size of a lotus leaf. "It's a snap," said Monkey, and jumped onto the Buddha's palm, before whizzing off on his magical cloud. Flying along for a great distance, he at last came to five fleshly pillars. Thinking that they must denote the limits of the world, he made a mark on the middle one and then returned. When Monkey reported the vast distance he had traveled, the Buddha laughed, and held out his hand. On his middle finger was the mark that Monkey had left. Monkey had not gone even a step beyond the limits of the Buddha's palm. This reflects the world of the *Flower Garland Sūtra*, where every phenomenon is located within the buddha-world.

Although Vairocana is the universe itself, transcending all forms and limits, he was strikingly expressed in symbolic human form within Mahāyāna Buddhism. The enormous Buddha figures at Bāmiyān reflect the idea of the Cosmic Buddha, and the tradition of making huge statues of the Buddha continued at Yün-kang in Shansi, China, and Tōdai-ji in Japan. The extreme of this symbolism came with the development of esoteric Buddhism, about which I refer readers to other reliable books.[6] Here I will discuss only the origin of esoteric *maṇḍalas,* geometric representations of the world that show the Buddha's manifold, far-reaching presence.

It is not known when the earliest Buddhist *maṇḍala* was made, but a depiction of a large number of buddha figures together is found in the "Miracle at Śrāvastī" relief (photo 5), though it does not follow a geometric pattern. There are, however, geometric depictions among the Buddha paintings at Bāmiyān in Afghanistan, as photo 11 illustrates.

I would argue that the origin of the *maṇḍala* is in cut glass, which features a pattern of round or hexagonal forms set into a goblet's rounded outer surface. If the glass is placed over a small object, such as a buddha figure, the figure appears within each form in the glass, just as in a *maṇḍala.* Such cut glass goblets have been discovered among the Kuṣāṇa remains at Begrām in Afghanistan, dated between the first and third centuries (photo 12 shows one example). The decorated, domelike ceilings of the rock-cut caves at Bāmiyān have similar features. As shown in photo 13, they give one the sensation of looking at cut glass from within; the decorations form a pattern of hexagons, each containing a buddha figure. It is tempting to think that the idea of the *maṇḍala* came about in this way.

The idea that the Buddha pervades the universe also appears in wall paintings of the thousand buddhas in Central Asia and at Tun-huang. Borobudur in Java is another mandala-type expression of *Flower Garland* thought (see photo 14). Six layers of square, graduated terraces are topped by a circular, three-tiered platform. One theory holds that the square section symbolizes the earth, and represents the realms of desire and form, whereas the upper round section represents the realm of formlessness. There are a total of 504 buddha figures, more than half of which represent the five buddhas of the Diamond Realm Mandala (Mahāvairocana, Akṣobhya, Ratnasaṃbhava, Amitāyus, and Amoghasiddhi). These encircle the stūpa in the center, which contains Mahāvairocana. This structure expresses the Mahāyāna idea that the buddhas emanate from Mahāvairocana and penetrate the universe, that the "one" is at the same time the "many." Borobudur was built in the eighth and ninth centuries, at much the same time as the great Buddha of Tōdai-ji in Nara, which indicates that *Flower Garland* concepts were prevalent throughout the Buddhist world at that time.

The *Flower Garland* worldview sees the Buddha in everything around us. Although pre-Mahāyāna Buddhism divided the world into the realms of delusion and enlightenment, and fostered a pessimistic outlook, Mahāyāna taught that the realm of delusion and the realm of the Buddha are inseparable, and thereby overcame that pessimism. The lotus flower, growing out of mud but not stained by it, is an apt symbol for this view of the world.

8. Changes in the Conception of Hell

The most significant transformation in the history of Buddhism is the shift from Hīnayāna to Mahāyāna Buddhism. But many smaller changes in religious thought also occurred over time and in a variety of places. This chapter discusses one prevalent example of this process: the idea of hell. The conception of hell underwent an evolution particularly in Japan, and was part of a kind of Japanization of Buddhism that began in the Heian period (794–1192 C.E.).

YAMA

In Japan, Emma (Yama in Sanskrit) is considered to be the lord of the underworld. We have seen in the *Abhidharmakośa,* though, that Yama's dwelling is in the sky above Mount Sumeru. Yama was originally a deity called Yamadeva, who more or less corresponded to the Brahmanic Yama of the *Ṛg Veda.* As we examine how Yama made his downward journey, we trace the development of the Buddhist idea of hell.

Let us examine what kind of deity Yama was initially, as described in the *Ṛg Veda.* According to this work (12th–8th century B.C.E.), the progenitors of the human race were twins, Yama and Yamī. Yamī, wanting descendants, urged Yama to join her in begetting offspring, but he refused, saying it was against human ethics. There was a bitter exchange between them, but the scriptures do not relate the outcome in any detail.

Considering the fact that the human race subsequently flourished, it seems that Yamī had her way. Yama, being the first man, was therefore the first person to die. He pioneered the way to the abode of the dead and became sovereign of that realm as others followed his path. His kingdom was in the heavens and was thought of as a kind of paradise.

Drawing upon the Brahmanic tradition, the Buddhist Yama also had his abode in the heavens. In the *Abhidharmakośa,* though, in addition to the heavenly Yama there is another Yama, who belongs to the realm of the hungry spirits. It is unclear whether these two are the same or different beings. What *is* obvious in the *Abhidharmakośa* is that the realm of the dead has shifted from the heavens to the underworld. This may have some connection with the historical shift from cremation to burial. It is thought that cremation was a custom of the Aryans, the composers of the *Ṛg Veda.* If we stretch the imagination, we could conjecture that burial was the norm of the people who occupied India before the Aryan invasion, and that the custom gradually reasserted itself in the face of Aryan pressure.

In any case, the realm of the dead, now having shifted to the subterranean abode of the hungry spirits, was no longer a pleasant and comfortable land, but a sad and gloomy place where the majority of the dead were forced to suffer. Even in the Vedic period there had been unhappy dead. Venerating the spirits of dead ancestors was an important duty of the descendants. Those who died without progeny had no one to enshrine them and so became unhappy spirits. (The description in the Chinese *Book of Rites* [Li-chi] that "a spirit is one who is dead and without a tomb" derives from the same type of thinking.) By the time of the *Abhidharmakośa* (5th century C.E.), a being unhappy in death was considered merely to have reaped what he had sown in life.

In Sanskrit an ancestral spirit is *pitṛ, pitar,* or *pitā* (*pitṛ* or *pitar* originally meant "father" and was related to the Latin *pater*) and a hungry spirit is *preta.* In the vernacular Prākrit language, though, both are *peta.* It is not at all strange, therefore, that in the vernacular the ancestral spirit became a hungry spirit and Yama, lord of the ancestral spirits (*pitṛ-pati*), became lord of the hungry spirits.

Though in the *Abhidharmakośa* Yama descended to the realm of the hungry spirits, he did not at first go as far as the hells. The hells had their wardens, but they did not have a lord. All the same, Yama was not without some connection with the hells, for it was he who ordered the *rākṣasas* (flesh-eating demons) to toss living beings into them. After the time of the *Abhidharmakośa,* Yama did descend to become the lord of the hells, his second demotion. We see this in the *Yogācārabhūmi-śāstra* (ca. 5th–6th century C.E.).

Keep in mind that, in Buddhist thinking, death is one of many forms of rebirth. The hells were not the final dwelling place, but a point along the way. Buddhism taught that the sufferings of hell came as a result of deeds done in life. The hells themselves were formed by the karma of living beings, and even their wardens were born there as a result of karma. There was no figure of absolute judgment, divorced from the karma of living beings. Yama's lordship of the hells is the result, and philosophical requirement, of the introduction of the idea of judgment into the Buddhist concept of hell. With judgment came the need for a judge, and before long the lord of the hungry spirits had taken over that role. At this point, in Japan, the transliterative character *-ma* of *Yama* was replaced with a frightful character meaning "demon."[1]

The provenance of the idea of judgment is a question worthy of examination. One possible source lies near at hand, in the *Avesta* (ca. 7th century B.C.E.), the scriptures of Zoroastrianism. Zoroaster says, "I ask you these things, Ahura [the Zoroastrian supreme god]; what does indeed occur and arrive? What debt do they pay for judgment to the pure, what to the wicked, when these [judgments] shall be concluded?"[2] The idea also appears in Greek mythology. Minos sits in judgment over the dead, as does Hades. In the *Odyssey* Homer describes Minos as "sitting, gold sceptre in hand, and delivering judgment to the dead, who sat or stood all around, putting their cases to him for decision within the House of Hades, to which the gate is wide."[3] Hades corrects humans in the underworld, recording all their deeds on a slate and investigating them. It is difficult to say which of these ideas of judgment is closest to the Buddhist concept, though graphically the Buddhist and Greek judges have many similarities. Both are depicted, in texts or in visual arts, as holding scepters and writing implements. In Judaism, of course, God is the judge. The Chinese concept of the other world must also be considered, as must the possibility that ideas from different cultures influenced Buddhism concurrently. Furthermore, we must not forget that all these ideas might have a common origin somewhere—for example, a picture from ancient Egypt that shows the heart of a dead person being measured is suggestive.

SANZU NO KAWA

A new and different aspect of hell entered Japanese Buddhism around the eleventh century. This was *Sanzu no kawa,* the "river of the three ways." In the history of ideas, seemingly incongruous ideas sometimes appear, whose origins are difficult to trace. Sanzu no kawa is one of these cases. The idea of a river that has to be crossed after death appears in literature as *watari-gawa* ("river to be crossed") in *The Great Mirror* (Ōkagami, ca. 1119), as *sanzu no kawa* ("river of the three ways") and *mitsuse-gawa* ("river of the three currents") in *The Rise and Fall of the Genji and Heike* (Gempei Seisuiki, fourteenth century), and as *sanzu no kawa* in the *Chronicle of the Great Peace* (Taiheiki, ca. 1371). Sanzu no kawa is not an orthodox Buddhist concept. There is absolutely no mention of it, for example, in the *Abhidharmakośa* or in later Indian Buddhist writings. Nor is there any Indic equivalent of the expression. Furthermore, it is an idea that appeared around the time Buddhism began to decline in India, when the creative activities of Buddhists had come to a standstill (ca. 10th century). This suggests that the idea entered Buddhism from another region, perhaps the border regions of India or somewhere in

China. Another possibility is that the idea arose within Buddhism itself at a later date.

The *Abhidharmakośa* mentions the existence of a sub-hell called Nadī Vaitaraṇī ("burning river"), as discussed in chapter 2. This hell takes the shape of a river or moat, and the name of this "burning river," Vaitaraṇī, has the connotation of "to cross." Perhaps this hell became a "river to be crossed" and was the forerunner of Sanzu no kawa. The two rivers differ, however, on the following three points. First, Nadī Vaitaraṇī is itself a hell, whereas the Sanzu no kawa stands at the entrance to the underworld. Second, Nadī Vaitaraṇī is a sub-hell, where the damned are tortured on leaving hell proper, and is therefore a hell to which people fall *after* entering hell proper. The Sanzu no kawa, on the other hand, has to be crossed *before* people enter hell. Third, there are four Nadī Vaitaraṇīs associated with each of the hot hells, making thirty-two in all. There is only one Sanzu no kawa.[4] Yet there are those who remain convinced that there is sufficient scope in the concept of Nadī Vaitaraṇī for Sanzu no kawa to have developed from it if a long period of time is taken into consideration.

There is the added possibility that if some other concept much closer to Sanzu no kawa happened to exist in or near a Buddhist region, that concept might have been adopted into Buddhism. In fact, both Greek mythology and the Zoroastrian scriptures contain descriptions of such a river. For purposes of comparison, let us first consider the description of Sanzu no kawa as it appears in Mochizuki's Buddhist dictionary, based on a sūtra called the *Sūtra of Kṣitigarbha Bodhisattva and the Ten Kings* (Jizō bosatsu hosshin innen jūō-kyō, ca. 12th century), probably composed in China or Japan.

> Near the Sōzuga [Sanzu no kawa], in the vicinity of Shokō, stretching together are the offices of the officials receiving those who cross. The great river in front is the Sōzuga. The dead who cross are called "forders of the river of hell." There are three crossing points: (1) the shoals of the upper stream

> [*sansui* in Japanese]; (2) the depths of the lower stream [*kōshin'en*]; and (3) the bridged crossing [*ukyōto*]. In front of the official building is a large tree, called *eryōju*. Two demons live in its shadow, one called Datsueba ["the old woman who rips off robes"], and the other Ken'eō ["the old man who hangs out robes"]. The female demon admonishes against thieving actions and breaks the fingers of both hands, and the male demon abhors lapses in ritual and bends the head against the feet. And men [who are first-time offenders in adultery] bear their women on their backs, and the ox-headed [demons who are the guardians of hell] bind the shoulders of two people with iron poles and chase them across the swift current. All gather under the tree. There the female demon rips off their robes and the male demon hangs the robes on the branches. They weigh their sins by the degree of bending [of the branch], then send them to the court of judgment.[5]

According to Greek mythology, there are five rivers in the underworld: Styx, Acheron, Cocytus (Kōkytos), Lethe, and Pyriphlegethon (Phlegethon). Because the *san* in Sanzu no kawa means "three," it might be thought that the five rivers of the underworld are unlikely ancestors of Sanzu no kawa. *San,* however, refers not to the number of rivers but to the number of crossing points on one river; furthermore, the Greeks did not consider five rivers to be a fixed number, and did not conceive them as a group of five at a particular time. More important is the fact that the Greek and Mochizuki's descriptions have in common the factor that the dead have to cross the river prior to entering the underworld. There are other similarities. There is a guard or ferryman at each river, with whom the dead have to negotiate when crossing. A ferryman called Charon carries the dead across the Acheron for a fee; in Japan, Datsueba and Ken'eō guard the Sanzu no kawa. It was a custom in both Greece and Japan to place a coin in the coffin or in the mouth of the dead person. It therefore seems reasonable to allow that the idea of the Acheron had some influence on the concept of Sanzu no kawa.

The Zoroastrian *Avesta* (ca. 7th century B.C.E.) describes the souls of the dead as crossing the Bridge of the Separator, Chinvato Peretu, before reaching the shore (*haētu*) of three Yazatas (angel-like beings). This bridge reminds us of the "bridged crossing" in Mochizuki's description of Sanzu no kawa. In the *Avesta,* however, it is the souls of the righteous who proceed across the Chinvat Bridge to the shore of the Yazatas, whereas the Sanzu no kawa is crossed only by evildoers and denotes a gloomy and melancholy place. The easy and safe "bridged crossing," unlike "the shoals of the upper stream" and "the depths of the lower stream," has no connotation of punishment; it thus may be related to the Chinvat Bridge. Interestingly, the Japanese Buddhist priest Nichiren (1222–82), in his *Treatise in Praise of Ten Kings* (Jūō sandan-shō), describes this bridge as being made of the seven precious stones, including gold and silver, and says that only the good are able to cross it.

Although it is possible to seek Sanzu no kawa's origins in Greece and Iran, we must not forget China, which may have been where Greek and Iranian mythology accreted to Buddhism. The *Sūtra of Kṣitigarbha Bodhisattva and the Ten Kings* is said to have been narrated by a man called Tsang-ch'uan, who also appears as the narrator of an earlier sūtra, the *Sūtra on Rebirth into the Pure Land and the Ten Kings* (Yoshū jūō shōshichi-kyō, Chinese apocrypha, ca. 10th century). He was said to have lived during the T'ang dynasty (618–907) in China. If the two sūtras were authentic, they would have had to be composed in India and translated ("narrated") by Tsang-ch'uan. An analysis of their content, however, indicates that both seem to have been written in China, first and foremost because of the extremely Chinese nature of the names of the ten kings (*jūō*) of the titles.

We saw earlier how in Greek myth the dead had to pay a fee to Charon to be transported across the Acheron. The custom of inserting "burial money" (*i-ch'ien*) inside the coffin of the dead person prevailed in China from around the second century, and by the T'ang dynasty "paper money," coin shapes drawn on paper, had come to be used instead. The idea that the dead proceeded to a place called the "yellow springs" seems to have come into being around the time of Tso-ch'uan's *Commentary on the Spring and Autumn Annals* (ca. 3d century B.C.E.), prior to the introduction of Buddhism to China.[6] It is likely that pre-Buddhist Chinese ideas of the other world had much influence on the Buddhist concept of hells. Incidentally, it is said that Taoism adopted its idea of hell from Buddhism.

SAI-NO-KAWARA AND KṢITIGARBHA BODHISATTVA

Yet another conception of hell is *Sai-no-kawara,* the "riverbank of suffering," and it is also a product of later Buddhism. Though it is situated somewhere near the entrance to hell, its connection with Sanzu no kawa is unclear, and texts do not state that Sai-no-kawara is the bank of Sanzu no kawa. The concept most likely originates in the "village of Sahi," a burial ground for the common people at the confluence of the Kamo and Katsura rivers in Kyoto. Its existence is mentioned in records dating back to the latter half of the ninth century.[7] These records also mention the custom of piling stones to make small mounds (stūpas) in memory of the dead. The original meaning of *Sahi* is unclear (it may mean "rust" [*sabi*] or "astringent" [*shibu*]), but later it appears to have become linked with the gods of boundaries (Sae no kami, or Dōso-jin), who prevent evil spirits from entering a village. Small shrines or piles of stones dedicated to them are placed at crossroads, and travelers add small stones to the mound in much the same way as travellers crossing the Tibetan passes. As crossroads and mountain passes are dividing points, Sai-no-kawara is the dividing point between the realms of the living and the dead.

Sai-no-kawara is notorious as a place of torture for children. It is said that a dead child caused its mother much pain and suffering while in the womb and yet died without returning any of the kindness it had received, and that it caused its parents to grieve by dying. Surely this is not the fault of the child, and indeed this would have been the cry of those who had lost their children. They would have felt no need for their children to repay any imaginary debts. All the same, in Buddhism everyone, including children, roams the realms of delusion as long as they have not reached enlightenment. Everyone passes through the six paths of transmigration, and who can say who eludes the torments of hell?

At Sai-no-kawara, children who die young have to build stone mounds without cease. Children of three or four, separated from their parents, are tormented by the guards of hell and forced to pile up small stones to make mounds. As soon as these mounds are almost finished, they are knocked down, and the children have to begin piling up stones all over again. This is the Japanese version of the Greek myth of Sisyphus, who for his crimes was hurled into Tartarus and condemned eternally to roll a large rock up a hill. As soon as the rock almost reached the top it would come hurtling down and Sisyphus would have to start his endeavors again. I am convinced that the myth of Sisyphus influenced the description of the piling up of rocks at Sai-no-karawa.

There is a famous poem (*wasan*) about Sai-no-kawara that deeply moves the Japanese, translated here in prose.

> We devote ourselves to the Three Treasures [Buddha; Dharma, or his teachings; and Saṅgha, or community of believers]. In this world all is transient. In the fact that children may die before their parents, there are various kinds of sadness. Young children, one or two, or three, or four, or younger than ten, are separated from their mother's breasts, gathered together on the riverbank of Sahi, where for all the hours of the day they carry big stones and pile them into mounds. For all the hours of the night they pick up small stones and pile them into stūpas. They pile the first layer [of

> stones] for Father, the second for Mother. On the third they face the west and place their tiny hands together, for their brothers and sisters in their native towns and themselves. Oh, how pitiful, young children crying and crying as they carry stones. Their hands and feet are lacerated by the stones, blood streams from their fingers, staining their bodies red. "I miss you, Father! I miss you, Mother!" Crying for their parents they fall down, crying as though they were in pain. The fearsome guards of hell, with their eyes like mirrors reflecting the sun, glare at the young ones. "The stupa mounds you have built are crooked and displeasing to the sight. They will bring you no merit as they are. Build them again, praying for your buddhahood." Thus howling at the children they flail their iron scourges and break down the stūpa mounds. The poor little children throw themselves down and weep. . . .
>
> A stream runs between the banks. The thought of the grieving parents in the Sahā world reaches there, and their shadows are reflected [on the stream]. Wishing to relieve their hunger, the children crawl and approach, longing for the [mother's] breast. At that moment [her] shade immediately disappears, and the [stream] water burns as bright as a flame, scorching the children's bodies, and the children fall down. Uncountable are such unbearable things.[8]

For parents who have lost young children, how sorrowful this poem must be! Not only have their beloved children gone to a place where the parents' hands and voices can no longer reach them but, unendurably, they are subjected to suffering at the riverbank. Moreover, if the parents mourn their children, their voices sound like the cries of demons to the children; the hot tears of the fathers become boiling water raining down on them, and the mothers' tears, ice, imprisoning them. There must be parents who would even act wrongfully in order to follow their children to hell. But such a wrong act may separate them even more.

It is Kṣitigarbha Bodhisattva who observed the suffering of

the inhabitants of the six paths of transmigration and who, having undergone myriads of years of religious training, now walks there, relieving pain. Like the *bhikṣu* (ordained priest) Dharmākara (the name of Amitābha Buddha before his enlightenment), Kṣitigarbha made a number of vows, resolving to bring deliverance to living beings. He appears in works of art dressed as a Buddhist novice or a young Buddhist ascetic with shaved head, emblematic of his hurry to arrive at the realms of suffering.

But doesn't Amitābha already provide deliverance to all those who call upon his name? This he does, but he is far away, ten myriads of hundreds of millions of buddha-lands to the west. Kṣitigarbha, on the other hand, sets no conditions and will save all those transmigrating among the six paths of rebirth who may not repent and call upon Amitābha, or who may not know of Amitābha's existence. Moreover, Kṣitigarbha has himself come to Jambudvīpa and walks among the beings in the six paths of rebirth. In particular he is found in the hells, especially at Sai-no-kawara where young children are suffering. He takes their hands, and like a kindly old priest playing ball with children in a temple garden, he speaks gently to them and plays games with them. He is the buddha of whom it is said "a buddha in hell."

This contrast between the roles of Amitābha and Kṣitigarbha was not designed from the beginning. Amitābha and Kṣitigarbha originally represented two distinct lines of belief. The three Pure Land sūtras that speak of Amitābha contain no clear depiction of hell; there are only scattered references. The name of Kṣitigarbha is nowhere to be found. Kṣitigarbha seems to have belonged to another stream of thought entirely, that of the *tathāgata-garbha,* "repository of buddhahood" inherent in all beings. The Sanskrit name *Kṣitigarbha* means "earth matrix." He stores within himself all merits, and brings them forth in various forms.

All Buddhism, whether pre-Mahāyāna or Mahāyāna, stresses the spirit of compassion. When the idea of judgment entered Buddhism (ca. 10th–11th century), a sense of compassion soon ameliorated that gruesome notion, and so Yama, the judge, was said to be a manifestation of Kṣitigarbha. Yama, it was taught, is not as fierce as his aspect suggests; he terrifies people as a skillful means to lead them to deliverance. Certain beings may learn from the horrors of hell and be encouraged to escape the round of birth and death. Pictures of the Ten Kings (who sentence the dead in the underworld) show the judges fiercely berating evildoers, with the compassionate face of Kṣitigarbha looming close behind them. The cult of Kṣitigarbha was flourishing in China by the seventh century.

The Pure Land of *Sukhāvatī* and hell are not to be found in this world. Nevertheless, throughout Japan there are places in the mountains with names like "plain of Amitābha" and "valley of hell." These originate mainly from the practices of the *yamabushi*, mountain ascetics who populated these regions and named the various features to provide a means of training themselves and teaching the common people. Nowadays, though, the expressions *jigoku* ("hell") and *Sai-no-kawara* are often used casually as the names of outdoor pools at hot-spring resorts. At some of these places, arbors even provide delectable views. Sai-no-kawara was originally written with the first character meaning "to block." A character with the same pronunciation, but meaning "to enshrine," later replaced it. At Kusatsu, a hot-spring resort north of Tokyo, I found Sai-no-kawara written with the first character meaning "west," also with the same pronunciation. This latest change has no doubt come about through association with the idea of the western paradise of Amitābha. According to Buddhism, though, hell and its riverbank are not somewhere in the west but beneath our land of Jambudvīpa.

For people of the Middle Ages, in both Japan and Europe, hell was very real. It is curious how close the two distant cultures came on this point. Between the Heian and Kamakura periods in Japan, that is, between the ninth and thirteenth centuries, the idea of an approaching period of the Decay of the Dharma (*mappō*) gained currency. Numerous books depicting the hells or the hungry spirits were produced, and many people placed their faith in rebirth in the Pure Land of Amitābha. In

Europe, also, the idea of the millennium became influential, and depictions of hell appeared in the cathedrals of Germany and France in the twelfth and thirteenth centuries.

Early in the twentieth century a French scholar discovered Buddhist remains at Haḍḍa in Afghanistan. The stucco sculptures of demons' heads he unearthed attracted considerable interest because of their similarities with the demons' faces found in European cathedrals. The Haḍḍa sculptures are much earlier than the European ones, dating from the fourth and fifth centuries, and with good reason might be considered the models for the carvings of demons found in Christian churches. Another scholar believes that both traditions derive from Roman art, products of the borderlands of the Roman Empire, and that the similarities between them indicate an indirect connection (the Haḍḍa sculptures are Greco-Roman in style). The demons in the stucco sculptures of Haḍḍa may or may not have some connection with the concept of hell; certainly later they came to be linked with the demons who populated hell. I do not know whether any depictions of the Buddhist hell existed in India, but excavations have unearthed such depictions in Central Asia, and the Central Asian images are similar to the pictures of hell drawn in Japan. It is those images that cause us to postulate a connection between Japan and Europe during the Middle Ages.

In this chapter we have deviated from our discussion of Buddhist cosmology in India proper. But studying the Buddhist thought of different regions suggests that Buddhist cosmology has been and can be a worldwide concern. In the next chapter I will discuss the cosmology from this point of view.

9. The Buddhist View of the Universe Today

Mythologizing an Experiential Universe

In many ways, Buddhism is a unique religion and worldview. Compared with the modern scientific view of the world, the Buddhist perspective is considerably colored by religious and practical concerns: it sees the natural world in terms of its relationship to human destiny. Unlike other religious interpretations—Christianity, for example—Buddhism does not see the hand of God in the existence of the universe, and is pessimistic, believing that suffering is intrinsic to the world. Many authors have already discussed those issues, and readers will reach their own conclusions about them through examining Buddhist cosmological concepts. Here I would like to offer a historical interpretation of Buddhist cosmology's development, based on the material we have covered so far.

We have seen how the Buddhist conception of the universe underwent numerous changes over time. If we view those shifts as changing responses to the problem of human suffering, we can see a steady progression in one direction: Buddhists gradually ceased to regard life as suffering. Inevitably the Buddhist worldview, originally based on the idea that suffering was inescapable, became increasingly irrelevant and eventually entered the realm of myth. Let us look at these changes in regard to suffering over three stages, following the structure of this book.

The first stage corresponds to the first four chapters. It is the classical view of pre-Mahāyāna Buddhism, from the time of Śākyamuni to Vasubandhu in the fifth century. According to the legend of the departure from the four gates, Śākyamuni left home and embarked on the religious path because of his encounter with the three major expressions of unhappiness: old age, sickness, and death. He came to see that all existence is subject to the repetition of birth and death, and that this is the root of existential suffering. During this period in history, people shared the idea that life itself was suffering, and that Mount Sumeru and Jambudvīpa were realms of suffering.

Buddhism taught that existential suffering would continue as long as ignorance reigned. The greatest ignorance is the idea that the self exists absolutely, and this is the source of all suffering. People's highest concern must therefore be to undertake religious practice in order to overcome that ignorance. Suffering was considered an urgent and personal problem, and the compulsion to escape that suffering urged them toward religious training and practice. The earliest and most important expression of these ideas was the doctrine of the Four Noble Truths: that suffering exists, that it has a cause, that there is a means to annihilate suffering, and that the Eightfold Path is that means. (The Eightfold Path consists of right view, right thinking, right speech, right action, right living, right effort, right mindfulness, and right concentration.) Conceptions of the heavens, karma, and transmigration also addressed the issue of suffering.

The second stage corresponds to the discussion of buddha-realms in chapters 5 through 7. The growth of the Buddhist idea of paradise took place around the first and second centuries C.E., with the rise of Mahāyāna Buddhism. By this time people no longer felt suffering to be so cruel, having discovered the possibility of pleasure even within a life of suffering. Human life, rather than being the painful force that compelled people to religious training, became a powerful temptation holding them back. People suspended attempts to reach enlightenment because, in Shinran's words, they could not abandon the old home of suffering amid the round of birth and death. The new world of enlightenment, deferred until after death, was paradise, Sukhāvatī. Even the idea of paradise, Buddha's pure land, was secularized, and depicted as replete with the joys and adornments of secular life. This was an entirely different spiritual expression than that of the first stage, which regarded existence as evil and considered "nothingness" an ideal state.

The third stage corresponds to chapter 8 and its treatment of the idea of hell. In Japan's Edo period (1603–1868), when material life became easier and rationalism gained influence, there appeared a completely new understanding of the nature of hell, involving a dilution of its terrors. Suffering was not so much personal as an abstract condition that was the fate of all humankind. A new optimism had arisen, one that did not regard existence as consisting only of suffering. As a result, religious training lost its urgency. Depictions of hell became mythological and were experienced as literary romanticism rather than as the stark truth of human existence.

As people gradually stopped thinking of suffering as a threat, Buddhist cosmology, which had been constructed on the terror of suffering, steadily lost its connection to everyday reality. What had originally been a living belief turned into myth. This process had already occurred in Greece before the beginning of the common era, with the mythologization of ancient religion.

In modern times, the idea of existential suffering has further weakened. Human life is no longer regarded as a realm of suffering but instead as a setting for the actualization of human happiness. Suffering has even been given a somewhat positive meaning. The words of Kumazawa Banzan (1619–91), a Confucian thinker of Edo-period Japan, "However greatly troubles mount, I will confront them with the limited force of my being," are those of a modern man who stands up fearlessly to face suffering, rather than the view of a traditional Buddhist, who seeks to escape suffering.[1]

The modern turnabout in Buddhist values is not limited to the question of suffering. Changes in the meanings of Buddhist terms highlight the trend. For instance, the Japanese word *akirameru,* "to clarify the truth," was originally the highest religious act in Buddhism, but it is now understood in a negative way, meaning "to abandon" or "to resign oneself to something." Similarly, *gaman,* "self-importance," something which formerly was to be overcome, is now used to mean "patience" or "endurance," as when parents urge their children to forbear crying. This process of devaluation has been apparent over the last two or three centuries, no doubt linked to changes in Japanese society and lifestyle. The introduction of Western science and first-hand knowledge of India exacerbated this tendency. Thus the authority of Buddhist cosmology gradually lost its force. The nativist (*Kokugaku*) scholars of the eighteenth and nineteenth centuries, who favored traditional Japanese ways of thinking and living, viewed Buddhism as a foreign religion. They attacked it ruthlessly, realizing that they were provided with a powerful counter-weapon if Buddhist cosmology were taught as doctrine.

Hirata Atsutane (1776–1843) was such a nativist scholar and a Shinto theologian. He undermined the traditional authority of *Tenjiku* (India) and laughed away belief in paradise (Sukhāvatī). Quoting the description in the *Smaller Sukhāvatī-vyūha* that Amitābha's Pure Land had both night and day, he suggested that paradise seemed to exist within our own world, being blessed with the sun and the moon. Of course no one had ever seen Sukhāvatī. It might, in fact, very well be Japan itself: because the world is round, if one keeps going farther and farther west one must reach Japan! He also ridiculed Buddhism, saying that a person sitting for a long time on a lotus flower in paradise might fall into the water when yawning as a result of boredom, or when sneezing because someone was talking about him or her back in the land of the living. Therefore, he quipped, people should learn to swim. If someone drowned by falling off a lotus flower, where would he or she be born next? he wondered.

Here we seem to have arrived at the terminus of Buddhist cosmology as a practical philosophy. It is a point all ancient views of the universe have finally reached. As knowledge is disseminated in ever-greater amounts, people have sought out the rational and overturned old dogmas. Yet Buddhist cosmology will not be completely forgotten, for within it reality became one with the realm of religion. Its vast cosmological system and its detailed explanations are unique. Buddhist cosmology is a spiritual legacy of the past, yet it remains a force capable of stirring the imagination of people today. Like old ceremonial garments no longer worn, it retains an attraction for us and can transport our minds to the spiritual world of ancient and medieval people, in the same way that the Greek myths, though they have lost their significance as a religion, continue to maintain their hold on our imagination.

What Buddhist Cosmology Teaches Us

Can new inspiration spring from Buddhist cosmology's ashes? Let us look first at the idea of transmigration. Many modern people view it as outmoded, but I believe that it has many points relevant to the world today. The body of a dead worm returns to the earth, and its constituents change and become grass. This grass is eaten and becomes part of a cow, and eventually people eat the cow. Then they, too, return to the earth and become worms. If we pursued a single atom of nitrogen, we would probably find that it circulated among Gosāla's 1,406,600 kinds of living beings. People are born, and people die. They experience a variety of emotions such as anger, love, and hate, and die with their minds unsettled. They are followed, in turn, by others beginning their lives of anger, love, and hate. Human life is thus full of such delusions, which actually have no absolute existence. Transmigration is the intuitive expression of this meaningless round of birth and death.

The quickest way to understand the Buddhist view that human life is delusion is to recognize it in one's own inner life. As many of us grow to adulthood, our inner hypocrisy and evil reveal their ugly selves. The repeated experience of feelings of confidence followed by subsequent disappointment causes even more suffering than experiencing disappointment alone. As we grow older, our youthful admiration for the nobility of life and for the achievements of human beings may die away. Though we may be moved by expressions of nature or human life, we cannot wholly reject the conviction that life is something like transmigration.

Many people will no doubt judge the idea of transmigration to be gloomy and life-negating. Those who consider the spiritual condition of Japan late in the Heian period (794–1185), when the idea of impermanence dominated thought, may take the position that Buddhism is retrogressive and harmful. Buddhism recognizes the realities of life (even if they are not what one might hope), and does not try to conceal reality that is unpleasant. Furthermore, the idea of transmigration does not necessarily lead to a nihilistic lifestyle.

One possible result of the idea of transmigration's development in Japan can be found in the contrast between the words *pessimism* and *nihilism*. It is difficult to differentiate the two clearly; let us interpret the former as "the rejection of this world as imperfect," and the latter as "the idea that everything is void." Pessimism regards this world as imperfect, but it does not deny everything. In these terms, Indian Buddhism is certainly pessimistic, for it denies that the reality of this world is anything more than transmigratory existence. But it has one clear purpose, liberation, and it sets out along a defined road, religious training. Transmigration and liberation from transmigration: these are the two wheels of the chariot of Indian Buddhism, indispensable to its view of human life.

In the *Nirvāṇa Sūtra* (ca. 3d–2d century B.C.E.), the final words of Śākyamuni were, "All things pass. Strive without ceasing to perfect your religious practice." Because all things pass, we must try to perfect our religious practice, and thus conquer the imperfect world. For Indian Buddhists, a pessimistic outlook was the force propelling them toward a high purpose. When this pessimistic view of humanity entered Japan, however, it became colored with nihilism. Buddhism, which in the Nara period (710–94) appears to have had ritualistic, political influence, during the Heian period came to imbue the spiritual life of the people. The phrase "the impermanence of all things" symbolizes the Buddhism of the eleventh and twelfth centuries, which focused on the pitiful nature of human life. This happened because Buddhism had forgotten its watchword, "strive without ceasing," and so had lost sight of its purpose. Why this happened is a tricky question.

One reason for the shift from pessimism to nihilism can be found in Mahāyāna Buddhism's own philosophy of emptiness (*śūnyatā*). In *śūnyatā* nothing was either bad or good. During the Heian period, this philosophy criticized pre-Mahāyāna Buddhism's dissatisfaction with the present. In one sense it was an attempt to bring into Buddhism a more optimistic attitude about life, but it turned out to be a paralyzing agent, taking away the certainty of all values. This weakened both the pre-Mahāyāna negation of the value of human life and Mahāyāna impulse to undertake religious training.

Another reason was the fact that Mahāyāna made inroads into Japanese society by attaching itself to the nobility and to literature. This period corresponds to the second of our three stages concerning the consciousness of suffering. While on the one hand the nobility held to the Buddhist teaching that human life is imperfect, they could materially afford to emphasize that which was beautiful and pleasant in life. Forgetting about work, the court nobility tended to separate themselves from real life and frolic in a world of the imagination. The vigorous lifestyle of Śākyamuni's time had abated, and the nobility held human life in greater esteem. Leisure opened a space in their minds, and in filling up that space they indulged their aesthetic consciousness. They drowned themselves in an atmosphere of aesthetics; to them anything, even death itself, was beautiful. A line from a poem by the Japanese Buddhist priest and poet Saigyō, "Let me die in spring under the blossoming trees, let it be around that full moon of Kisaragi month [the second month of the lunar year]," is an expression of this sentiment.[2] In this nihilism, values are uncertain and all is void. The secularized Buddhism of the late Heian period certainly lost the goal of liberation from existence and in particular the path to it. (In this sense we can say that the sect founders of the Kamakura period [1185–1336], such as Shinran [1173–1262], Dōgen [1200–1253], and Nichiren [1222–82], reaffirmed the path, that is, religious practice.)

Purpose is meaningless without the path to its achievement. According to Zen, the purpose is liberation, and the path is religious practice (*zazen,* "sitting meditation"). According to the Pure Land sects, the purpose is salvation (Pure Land rebirth) and the path is recitation of Amitābha's name (*nembutsu*). There are other paths in Buddhism, however. Zen says that "the mind of everyday life is in itself the path." I understand this to mean that rather than actively trying to escape the river of transmigration, one should trust oneself to the flow; in other words, one should rid oneself of ego-attachment. In this way, everyday life takes on a new dimension. Absorbed in daily existence, the mind becomes conscious that somewhere there exists something of higher value. The more we penetrate transmigratory existence (human life), the more brilliantly that beacon shines above us. It is because of that higher existence that we can be of settled mind regarding transmigration and entrust ourselves to it. For those who do not know such a higher existence, the present life is all, and despair forever looms before them. Only those who do not cling to their own existence are able to view the world with equanimity, never finding disappointment. Paradoxically, it is then that the world seems acceptable. This may be a pessimistic outlook, but it is not nihilistic.

An antidotal practice for transmigration, meditation (*dhyāna*), can also teach the modern person much. As we have seen, Buddhism regards the variegated world as a realm of illusion, amplified by the activity of the sense organs. Liberation therefore begins with the control of those organs by means of meditation. Gradually the spirit becomes unified, and a single world comes into being, in which there is no distinction between you and me, good and bad, happy and unhappy.

Advanced Buddhist philosophy was born of the practice of meditation. On occasion it compares favorably even with Western philosophy. Coming to the conclusion that all could be doubted except his own existence, the French philosopher and mathematician René Descartes (1596–1650) said, "I think, therefore I am" (*Cogito ergo sum*). Buddhism goes still further in linking the questions of existence and mind (or consciousness). The existence of the world is identified with *ego,* "I." *Sum,* "I am," however, is merely one defined stage. Searching for this *ego* more deeply, seeking the roots of existence, we gradually reach the higher levels of the abode of the infinity of consciousness, the abode of nothingness, and the abode of neither thought nor non-thought. Farther than that is beyond the boundaries of language.

Let us next examine Buddhist cosmology itself in terms of its modern significance. There are a surprising number of similarities between Buddhist cosmology and modern science. We have seen how Buddhism regards the world as a plurality, coming into being and then disintegrating over a long period of time, a process which continues infinitely into the past and the future. Numbers concerning space and time increase in geometric ratio, and the field of vision concerning the universe, in terms of the very small and the very large, expands virtually to infinity. If we remove the graphic, the dogmatic, and the mythological from the expressions of Buddhist cosmologists, we are left with a series of concepts that resemble in no small way the conclusions of modern science. We may include here ideas such as the solar and galactic systems, the birth and extinction of nebulae, the birth of the heavenly bodies from cosmic dust, and the concept of thousands and billions of light years. If we translate the words of two thousand years ago into our modern tongue, it becomes apparent that Buddhist and modern cosmology are not all that far apart.

The ideas of hell and paradise can also be explained in terms of Buddhist symbolism. We saw previously how the human realm, as well as the realm of the underworld, is created by the karmic force generated by living beings. In the majority of cases, this karmic force is created blindly; karma breeds karma, and in a mass called "common karma" causes results shared by many, an unpredictable or at least unopposable fate. For all we know, the country we inhabit, or the whole world for that matter, may suddenly turn into hell. Think, for example, how readily we are inclined to describe certain conditions as "hellish"; traffic may be "hell," or the daily commute, and in Japan the competition engendered by annual examinations to enter high school or university is termed "examination hell." In the same way we can recover the truth of the Buddhist paradise. Paradise is a place where flowers bloom, birds sing, and the murmuring of a stream can be heard. Though we tend to dismiss paradise as an oversimplified concept, we would do well to consider, now that we are in danger of losing these things through environmental deterioration, that they do indeed represent paradise.

I would like to conclude by considering one further point, the possibility of the unification of science and religion. Though a great deal of time has passed since their separation began to be thought a problem, there seems to be no prospect of their reconciliation in the near future. This has led many people, particularly those speaking for religion, to assert that science and cosmology should deal with different dimensions. I cannot help having the impression that those advocates are acting out of a sense of self-preservation in light of the truths that science is revealing.

Nevertheless, science seems to have been won over by those voices, and has imposed on itself a taboo on discussing the meaning of human life and happiness. Faced with such contradictory (or at the least, disunified) ideas, can human beings attain happiness? The answer is no. To think that science and religion should deal with different dimensions is superstition. People must have only a single, unified understanding of the world if they are to live in faith.

Buddhist cosmology skillfully combines the scientific and the religious, unremittingly concerned with the nature of human suffering and deliverance from that suffering. Modern cosmologies have forgotten about the happiness factor, but Buddhism never has. Of course, many of the scientific elements in Buddhist cosmology have become outdated as a result of scientific progress, and so have lost their usefulness. But its science is not dogma, and it can change at any time according to new knowledge. The religious ideas of karma and rebirth, suffering and deliverance, are completely compatible with the new science. I do not know what new understanding of the world will arise in the future, but the existence of Buddhist cosmology points to the possibility of a new worldview that unites science and religion.

APPENDIX

Linear Measurement

The smallest linear measurement unit used by the ancient Indians is the atom (*paramāṇu*), the smallest indivisible particle of matter. When seven of these join together, the unit is called an *aṇu,* meaning "minute." Seven of these together make a "gold dust mote" (*loha-rajas*). (Gold was evidently thought to be very fine and its particles therefore very small.) Seven "gold dust motes" make a "water droplet" (*ab-rajas*), considered the smallest particle of water. Seven "water droplets" in turn make a speck of dust equal to the width of the tip of a strand of hare's fur (*śaśa-rajas*), which is known to be extremely fine. The next unit, comprising seven of these, is a speck of dust equal to the width of the tip of a sheep's hair (*avi-rajas*), and a collection of seven of these makes a speck that equals the width of the tip of a cow's hair (*go-rajas*). These are followed in size by a dust mote seen in a ray of sunlight coming through a chink in a wall (*chidra-rajas*). Seven of these become a "louse egg" (*likṣā*), and seven "louse eggs" are in turn considered to be a "louse" (*yūka*) in size. Seven "lice" are a "kernel of barley" (*yava*) and seven "kernels of barley" are an *aṅgulī-parvan,* a "finger joint," which means the distance between two joints of a finger.

The next unit of measurement is the *hasta,* "forearm," which refers to the distance between the tip of the fingers and the elbow. The size of a *hasta* is twenty-four times the width of a finger, a testament to the powers of close observation possessed by Indians. Next in size to the *hasta* is the *dhanus,* a "bow." The bow was one of the weapons the Indians used in war; it is close to four times as long as the *hasta.* The bow-length is also called *vyāma,* which means "to extend or stretch." The Chinese translated this with a character that now means "to seek or investigate" and which seems to signify the distance between the fingertips of a person's arms stretched out to the sides. Modern dictionaries translate the term as *fathom,* a word also originally meaning "the space reached by the extended arms."

The unit next in size to the *dhanus* is the *krośa,* the length of five hundred bows lined up lengthwise. Originally *krośa* signified the sound of a cow mooing; the length is therefore the distance at which a cow can be heard. Buddhists, however, gave it a more personal interpretation—the distance between the forest and a village. Many Buddhists lived in forests much of the time, performing their religious training; at mealtime, though, they would take their alms bowls and seek food in a nearby village. The regulations, in fact, stipulated that a Buddhist practitioner should not live too near to, or too far from, a village; if too near, they would be bothered by the village lifestyle, and if too far, they would not be able to get to the village easily to beg for food. The ideal distance was considered to be one *krośa.*

The final unit is the *yojana.* This word originally signified "being yoked"; it is, in fact, etymologically related to the English yoke. The distance a cow yoked to a cart could pull was one *yojana.* It consists of eight *krośas.*

A study of Indian units of measurement gives us some idea of the lifestyle of the ancient Indians. Villages lay close to the forest. Cows, prized for their milk, could be heard in the distance or seen pulling carts. Barley was grown. At times the soldiers of the king would appear on the main thoroughfare of the village, armed with bows. Perhaps people sat in sunny corners and picked off lice. They were familiar with rabbits and sheep.

Let us compare the traditional measurements to those used today. The *paramāṇu* and the "golden dust mote," etc., corresponding to our atoms and molecules, are too small and abstract to be calculated. The *dhanus* ("bow") would be roughly a body length, approximately two meters. Five hundred of them make a *krośa,* about one kilometer, the distance a cow can be heard. The *yojana* would, by the same reckoning, be eight kilometers; probably, though, the length is closer to seven kilometers because we have slightly overestimated the length of the *dhanus*.

Notes

Chapter 1

1. The *Abhidharmakośa* has two parts: a verse section (the *Abhidharmakośa-kārikā*), which is a condensed commentary on doctrine; and a prose section (the *Abhidharmakośabhāṣya*), which is a fuller treatment of the same material. In this book I have made no distinction between the sections, referring to them both as the *Abhidharmakośa*. A good English translation of the *Abhidharmakośa* appeared after I had written my books on Buddhist cosmology. This is *Abhidharmakośabhāṣyam by Louis de La Vallée Poussin,* vols. 1–4, trans. Leo M. Pruden (Berkeley, Calif.: Asian Humanities Press, 1988–90). The chapter on the world is included in volume 2.

2. *Abhidharma-mahāvibhāṣā-śāstra* (Great Commentary), vol. 136, *Taishō Tripiṭaka,* vol. 27 (Tokyo: Daizō Shuppan, 1924–29), p. 702a.

3. Hajime Nakamura, *Indo Shisō Shi* (History of Indian thought), 2d ed. (Tokyo: Iwanami Shoten, 1968), 42.

4. Louis Renou and Jean Filliozat, *L'Inde Classique: Manuel des études indiennes,* vol. 2 (Paris: École Française d'Extrême-Orient, 1953).

5. Each of the seven concentric mountains around Mount Sumeru, except Sudarśana ("looking good"), has a distinctive name. Yugandhara means "maintaining a yoke." Īṣādhāra means "maintaining a shaft." Khadiraka is the name of a well-known hardwood. Aśvakarṇa is the name of a tree whose leaves are shaped like horses' ears. Nimindhara means "maintaining a circle," and Cakravāḍa means "maintaining a wheel," (for *vāda,* refer to the Hindu *vālā,* "be possessed of"). Thus the names of the seven ranges are nearly all related to vehicles or to the material that was perhaps used to construct them.

Some have suggested that the Chinese translation of *vinataka* as "elephant's ears" might be a mistake for the Indic word for "elephant's trunk." The original Sanskrit text of the *Abhidharmakośa* (*Abhidharmakośa-bhāṣya,* ed. P. Pradhan, 1st ed. [Patna: K. P. Jayaswal Research Institute, 1967], p. 159) gives the original word as *vinitaka,* which, however, does not appear in any dictionary. *Vinataka* means "bowed" or "bent." In Paramārtha's Chinese translation of the *Abhidharmakośa, Chü-she-shih lun* (*Taishō Tripiṭaka,* vol. 29, p. 214b), and Hsüan-tsang's translation, *Chü-she lun* (*Taishō Tripiṭaka,* vol. 29, p. 57b), the term is transliterated as *p'i-na-to-k'o* and *p'i-na-ta-chia,* respectively. In Tibetan translations it appears as *rnam ḥdus,* a mechanical transposition of *vinataka* into Tibetan, and means "bowed" or "bent." The translation into meaningful Chinese characters appears as "elephant's ears" in Susumu Yamaguchi and Issai Funabashi, *Kusharon no Genten Kaimei* (Translation and annotation of the Sanskrit text of the *Abhidharmakośa*), chapter on the world ([Kyoto: Hōzōkan, 1955], p. 365), and as "elephant's trunk" in Mochizuki's Buddhist dictionary (*Bukkyō Dai Jiten*), vol. 3 (Tokyo: Sekai Seiten Kankō Kyōkai, 1933, p. 2515a).

In Hinduism, Vināyaka is the god Gaṇeśa (see chapter 6, pp. 140–41). Depicted in the form of an elephant, he has a long trunk and large ears. The Buddhist expressions "elephant's ears" and "elephant's trunk" may be terms born of a confusion between *vinitaka* (*vinataka*) and *vināyaka.* However, there is nothing in the meaning of either *vināyaka* or *gaṇeśa* that gives a clue to the Chinese translation's use of the characters for ears or trunk. *Vināyaka* means no more than "leader," while *gaṇeśa* means "lord of the herd." Etymology aside, it is tempting to say that *vinitaka* should be translated as "elephant's trunk," because we already have "horse's ears" (*aśvakarṇa*), the name of the concentric mountain, which contrasts nicely with "elephant's trunk." Furthermore, the elephant's popular name *hastin,* derived from "nose," shows that the elephant's prominent characteristic is its trunk rather than its ears. For the time being, however, I will leave *vinitaka* (*vinataka*) as "elephant's ears."

Another word similar to *vinitaka* is *vinītaka* (= *vainītaka*), which means "palanquin" or "litter." Considering that many of the names of the mountains are connected with vehicles, it is possible that the name of the mountain range under question might be Vinītaka. If this is so, its name should then be translated as Mount Palanquin.

6. If we based our calculations on the values given in figure 6, the

diameter of the golden earth layer would be 1,200,875 *yojanas,* not the 1,203,450 *yojanas* given in our initial description. Yaśomitra's commentary on the *Abhidharmakośa,* the *Abhidharmakośavyākhyā* (extant in Sanskrit [*Sphuṭârthā: Abhidharmakośavyākhyā by Yaśomitra,* parts 1 and 2, ed. Unrai Wogihara (Tokyo: Sankibō Buddhist Book Store, 1971)]) and Tibetan, ca. 5th or 6th century C.E.), sets out a number of opinions on this matter. One is that the width of the outer sea is not 322,000 *yojanas* but rather 1,287.5 *yojanas* greater. Another is that the golden earth layer extends beyond the Iron Mountains by the amount of the deficit. Still another is that the cross section of the mountains is not a true rectangle but more trapezoidal in shape (that is, the width of the mountains is only approximately the same as their height above the water), and when we add the length of the base of the mountains, the total is greater than 1,200,875 *yojanas.* Yaśomitra himself seems to favor the second interpretation.

7. In Japan there is a mountain called Myōkō, which is a translation of Sumeru, *myō* being equivalent to *su* and *kō* ("tall") perhaps being equivalent to *meru.*

8. P. B. Spooner, "Zoroastrian period of Indian history," *Journal of the Royal Asiatic Society* (1915): 407f.

9. "Dionysus named this city Nysa and this land Nysaea in memory of his nurse, who bore that name; and to the mountain near the city he gave the name Merus—or the Thigh—because legend has it that he grew in the thigh of Zeus." Arrian, *Campaigns of Alexander,* bk. 5, sec. 2, trans. Aubrey de Sélincourt (Harmondsworth, England: Penguin Books, 1987), 256.

10. It is said, however, that both the Egyptians and the Chaldeans believed in the sun's horizontal-plane movement. W. F. Warren, "Problems still unsolved in Indo-Aryan cosmology," *Journal of the American Oriental Society* 26 (1905): 86–87.

11. P. Mus, "Barabudur, les origines du stūpa et la transmigration," *Bulletin de l'École Française d'Extrême-Orient,* tome 32, fasc. 1 (1932): 384.

12. The Wheel of the Dharma (*dharma-cakra* in Sanksrit) refers to Śākyamuni Buddha's teachings, which are compared to the wheel-rolling king's wheel treasure because they crush all the evils of living beings. (A wheel-rolling king is any king who is strong and sacred, and the wheel treasure symbolizes kingly power or religious truth.) They are also like a wheel in motion because they spread endlessly from one person to another.

13. According to the *Great Commentary* (vol. 5, p. 701c), they run clockwise, which agrees with the Buddhist idea that movement around a holy object should be in a clockwise direction. The compiler of the *Abhidharmakośa,* a kind of abridged version of the *Great Commentary,* may also have thought that the rivers ran clockwise.

14. Yutaka Iwamoto, *Gokuraku to Jigoku* (Paradise and hells) (Tokyo: San'ichi Shobō, 1965), 23–24.

15. Mochizuki, *Bukkyō Dai Jiten,* vol. 3, 2934.

16. According to the *Abhidharmakośa,* living beings (*sattva*) inhabit the sun and the moon, under the jurisdiction of the Four Great Kings (see chapter 2). Folk legend has it that a rabbit inhabits the moon. Let us examine this legend from the *Records of the Western Regions of the Great T'ang Dynasty* (Ta-T'ang hsi-yü-chi), *Taishō Tripiṭaka,* vol. 51, p. 907b. Cf. *Si-yu-ki: Buddhist Records of the Western World,* trans. Samuel Beal (Delhi: Oriental Books Reprint Corp., 1969, pp. 59–60).

> Long ago, in a certain forest, there lived in great amity a fox, a monkey, and a rabbit. Thinking to test the hearts of the three animals, the god Indra took on the guise of an old man and appeared before them. "Are you well," he asked, "are you on good terms with one another?" The animals replied, "We are on very good terms." Then Indra said, "I came here because I had heard of your reputation for compassion. I am very hungry; won't you bring me something to eat?" The three animals immediately went off to search for food.
>
> The fox brought a carp from the river. The monkey brought fruit from a tree. Only the rabbit returned empty-handed and in consternation. Indra said, "Still your minds are not as one. You still lack religious training, for only the rabbit has brought me nothing." Then the rabbit said to the others, "Gather together firewood, lots of it. I have an idea."
>
> The fox and the monkey ran off and gathered dried grass and wood. The rabbit set fire to the wood, and said to Indra, "Old man, I have no strength and could bring you nothing to eat. Therefore, be pleased to make a meal of my body!" He threw himself on the fire and was burned to death. Indra returned to his true form, lifted the dead rabbit out of the fire, and with a great sigh said, "What kind feelings you had, and how you took it to heart! I will place the

rabbit in the moon so that future generations will know of this event." After that, there came to be a rabbit in the moon.

According to the *Records of the Western Regions of the Great T'ang Dynasty*, the name India signifies the moon (*indu*). This is a later theory, however, and there seems to be no connection between the words *India* and *indu*. When the Chinese first heard about India, they called it Chuan-tu or T'ien-chu, both of which are transliterations of *Sindhu*, *Hindhu*, or some corrupted form of these words. Later Hsüan-tsang stated that neither "Chuan-tu" nor "T'ien-chu" was a correct pronunciation of the original word, which he wrote as *Yin-tu*. This form, pronounced "Indo" in Japanese, is still used today and thus is not a loanword from English or French.

Sindhu, *Hindhu*, and *India* are all derived from *Indus*, the name of the great river in the northwest of the subcontinent, and the name the Persians and Greeks gave to the basin of the Indus river. Later "India" grew to include the east and south. *Sindhu* appears to be a common noun, originally denoting "river." According to E. D. Phillips,

> People with Indo-European names ruled the Mitannian Kingdom in northern Iraq and Syria in the middle of the second millennium. Others passed on through Iran to found the Sanskrit-speaking Aryan society of India. Corded pottery found in the stone cist-graves of Kayakent near Derbent has been claimed as evidence that the Aryans passed the Caucasus by this route along the Caspian coast. Some Indo-European names of Mitannian kings appear with Caucasian suffixes in Hittite texts. The name of the ancient Sindians of the Kuban delta may be the Sanskrit *sindhava*, "men of the river." It is suggested that these Indo-Europeans remained in their old home when the majority passed southward, to arrive eventually on the banks of another river that they likewise called Sindhu and we call the Indus (E. D. Phillips, *The Royal Hordes: Nomad Peoples of the Steppes* [London: Thames and Hudson, 1965], 42).

Why then in later times did the theory arise that *India* meant "moon"? As we saw above, India was thought to be superior to all other countries in terms of religion. Hsüan-tsang explained that all living beings ceaselessly journey on the round of transmigration and rebirth through the long night of ignorance. In that darkness, India is a beacon; her sages, like the moon, guide the world. Though the stars shine, the cool moon is much brighter. Therefore India was eulogistically called *indu*, the moon.

17. Many mythologies from all over the world incorporate the motif of the sun and moon gods riding through the sky in their chariots. From the Middle East to India, we find paintings and carvings of the sun god driving a chariot with four horses. The thirteenth-century Sūrya temple at Konārak in eastern India, a Hindu temple famous for its erotic carvings, is dedicated to the sun god Sūrya and was conceived as a great wheeled chariot. Thus the sanctuary and *maṇḍapa* (temple) are called *vimāna*.

18. *Abhidharmakośa*, lines 12–13, p. 59b.

19. *Abhidharmakośabhāṣyam*, vol. 2, trans. Leo M. Pruden (Berkeley, Calif.: Asian Humanities Press, 1988), 461–62.

20. P. Pradhan, ed. *Abhidharmakośabhāṣyam of Vasubandhu*, 1st ed. (Patna: K. P. Jayaswal Research Institute, 1967), p. 166, line 17.

Chapter 2

1. Before Buddhism entered China, no such word existed in Chinese. It was transliterated as *nai-lo* (*naraku* in Japanese), and translated as *ti-yu* (*jigoku* in Japanese), "prison beneath."

2. *The Verses on the Law* (Dhammapada), *The Dhammapada: The Path of Perfection*, trans. Juan Mascaró (Harmondsworth: Penguin Books, 1973), 53. Parenthetical numbers following quotations refer to verse or line numbers in the source.

3. "Great good-fortune," *The Group of Discourses* (Sutta-nipāta), vol. 2, trans. K. R. Norman (Oxford: The Pali Text Society, 1992), 31.

4. "Kokāliya," *The Group of Discourses*, vol. 2, 76.

5. *Great Dictionary of the Meaning of Buddhist Terms* (Mahāvyutpatti), 7797, 7798, 7926, 7927. This dictionary categorizes many kinds of words according to numbered themes.

6. *The Mahābhārata*, vol. 19, ed. V. S. Sukthankar and S. K. Belvalkar (Poona: Bhandarkar Oriental Research Institute, 1959), Svargārohaṇa-parvan (chapter on the ascent to heaven), verses 16–25, pp. 8–9.

7. "Kokāliya," 77. Following are verses 667–75.

He goes to the place of impaling upon iron spikes, to the iron stake with its sharp blade. Then there is food like a ball of heated iron, thus appropriate.

(The hell-keepers) when they speak do not speak pleasantly. (The hell-dwellers) do not hasten towards them; they are not arriving at a refuge. They lie on scattered coals; they enter a blazing mass of fire.

And tying them up with a net (the hell-keepers) strike them there with hammers made of iron. (The hell-dwellers) come to blind darkness indeed, for it is spread out like mist.

Then moreover they enter pot(s) made of copper, a blazing mass of fire. In those they are indeed cooked for a long time, jumping up and down in the masses of fire.

Then the doer of wrong is cooked there in a mixture of pus and blood. Whatever region he inhabits, there he festers, as he is touched.

The doer of wrong is cooked there in water which is the abode of worms. There is not even a shore to go to (for refuge), for the cooking pots all around are all the same.

Moreover they enter that sharp Asipatta wood, (and) their limbs are cut to pieces. Seizing their tongue(s) with a hook, pulling them backwards and forwards, (the hell-keepers) strike (them).

Then moreover they approach Vetaraṇī, difficult to cross, with sharp blades (and) with razors (in it). Fools fall there-in, evil-doers, having done evil deeds.

There black and spotted dogs, and flocks of ravens, (and) greedy jackals indeed devour them, as they are wailing, (and) vultures and crows strike them.

8. Manu, *The Laws of Manu,* ch. 4, trans. G. Bühler, vol. 25 of Sacred Books of the East (Delhi: Motilal Banarsidass, 1964), 142–43. The mythological author of this work was Manu, or Original Man. It includes cosmography and cosmogony. Verses 88–90 in chapter 4 mention twenty hells. They are Tāmisra, Andhatāmisra, Mahāraurava, Raurava, Kālasūtra, Mahānaraka, Saṃjīvana, Mahāvīci, Tapana, Saṃpratāpana, Saṃhāta, Sakākola, Kuḍmala, Pūtimṛttika, Lohaśaṃku, Ṛjīṣa, Pathin, Śālmalī, Asipatravana, and Lohadāraka. The name of the remaining hell is uncertain; it may be either naraka or nadī. The term *naraka* in *The Laws of Manu* seems to denote both hells in general and a particular hell (Cf. *The Vishṇu Purāṇa: A System of Hindu Mythology and Tradition,* vol. 5, part 2, trans. H. H. Wilson, ed. Fitzedward Hall

[London: Trübner and Co., 1877], index [*naraka*]). *Nadī* ("river") is generally believed to refer to the Śālmalī nadī. The *śālmalī* is a tree with thorns, and the Śālmalī nadī may be a river with such trees on its banks or one whose water is an irritant.

9. Ibid., ch. 12, 500.

10. *Sūtrakṛtāṅga Sūtra,* bk. 1, lec. 5, ch. 1, in *Jaina Sūtras,* part 2, trans. Hermann Jacobi, vol. 45 of Sacred Books of the East, 279–81.

11. Ibid., ch. 2, 283–86.

12. *Uttarādhyayana Sūtra,* lec. 19, in *Jaina Sūtras,* part 2, 94–95.

13. There are doubts, however, whether *avīci,* which was translated into Chinese as "no interval," really does mean that. It is possible that the original meaning had been forgotten, and that the element *a,* which can be the negative in Sanskrit, was translated as *wu* ("no") in Chinese and that the second element was translated in a seemingly consistent way.

14. Genshin, *Ōjō Yōshū,* a modern Japanese translation by Mizumaro Ishida, Tōyō Bunko series (Tokyo: Heibonsha, 1963), 16–18.

15. P'u-kuang, *Chü-she-lun kuang-chi,* 30 vols., *Taishō Tripiṭaka,* vol. 41, no. 1821.

16. *Abhidharmakośa,* lines 11–12, p. 59a.

17. In Buddhism, the Chinese word *t'ien* (*ten* in Japanese) that we use to translate the Sanskrit *deva* ("heaven") does not indicate the sky, but the god. For example, *Bon-ten* denotes Brahmā as the king of the Brahmā heaven, and *Taishaku-ten* denotes Indra as the king of the Tuṣita heaven. The Indic *deva* is related to the Latin *deus* (god). Incidentally, when Christianity first came to Japan at the end of the sixteenth century, *deus* was transliterated into Japanese as *Daius.* No one knew that this was related etymologically to *Devadatta,* once a follower of the Buddha but later his great enemy. If Buddhists had realized this, they might have believed that Daius (Jesus Christ) was the reincarnation of Devadatta. The Chinese translated *deva* as *t'ien* ("heaven") perhaps because their own word for "god" (*shen*) had connotations of "spirit" for the Chinese.

The Indic *deva* refers to the divinity, and *deva-gati* refers to the place where divinities reside. In Chinese, however, *t'ien* can sometimes refer to both. The Indic noun and its derivatives were virtually the same form, and the Chinese tended to translate them using the same character. For example, they translated both *trayas-triṃśāḥ* ("the heaven of the thirty-three gods") and *trāyas-triṃśāḥ* ("the inhabitants of the heaven of the thirty-three gods") using exactly the same compound.

18. *Abhidharmakośa,* lines 11–12, p. 60b.

Chapter 3

1. Both these theories rejected other theories. The *Great Commentary* states, "Members of other schools added the *asura* to make six destinations of rebirth. This should not be done, for the sūtras teach only five destinations" (no. 1545, p. 868b). On the other hand, the *Commentary on the Great Perfection of Wisdom Sūtra* says, "The Buddha did not state clearly that there are five destinations of rebirth. The idea of five destinations is the theory of the Sarvāstivādins, whereas that of six belongs to the Vātsīputrīyas [one of the twenty Hīnayāna schools]" ([Ta-chih-tu-lun], 100 vols., attributed to Nāgārjuna [ca. 150–ca. 250 C.E.]; Kumārajīva's Chinese translation, *Taishō Tripiṭaka,* vol. 25, no. 1509, p. 135c).

2. *Sūtra of Cause and Effect in the Past and Present* (Kuo-ch'u-hsien-tsai-yin-kuo-ching), Guṇabhadra's Chinese translation, *Taishō Tripiṭaka,* vol. 3, no. 189.

3. For Buddhists, the doctrine of karma is extremely important. The following question in the *Abhidharmakośa* could not have been conceived by one not deeply concerned with karma. "Are the guards of hell [*naraka-pāla*] living beings or not?" (p. 58c). Those who fall into the hells and who suffer as hungry spirits are all living beings. But have the guards of hell, who torture the beings there, also been reborn there through karma? The *Abhidharmakośa* offers two explanations. The first is that the guards of hell are not living beings. Can things not classified as living beings act? The *Abhidharmakośa* says that they act by means of the karmic force of those that are living beings. The other explanation is that they are living beings, but unlike other beings their bodies have been specially made to withstand the fires of hell, and therefore do not burn. The evil a guard does finds retribution in the same hell in a future life.

4. *Sāmaññaphala-sutta.* Cf. *Dialogues of the Buddha,* vol. 2, trans. T. W. Rhys Davids, vol. 2 of Sacred Books of the Buddhists, (London: Pali Text Society, 1977 [1899]), 72. These numbers require some clarification. Gosāla seems to have held to an animistic way of thinking, for he

saw a spirit in the trees and grass, in seeds, in stones, and in water, resulting in 1,406,600 kinds of living beings. He also gives different kinds of karma. The large number, 500, seems to refer to all types, and the smaller numbers, 5, 3, 1, and ½, to specific categories. For example, the designation of five karmas probably refers to the actions based on sight, hearing, smell, taste, and touch; the three karmas to the three actions of body, speech, and mind; the one karma to action of the body or of speech; and the half karma to the mind, because the karma of the mind is as yet unrealized. The six classes are the black, blue, red, yellow, white, and pure white. The black is the class of people like fishermen and robbers who are concerned with evil actions (fishermen take life). The blue are the practitioners of Buddhism, the red the followers of Jainism, the yellow those who follow the Ājīvikas, the white the ordained men and women of the Ājīvikas, and the pure white the three leaders of the Ājīvikas, including Gosāla.

The eight stages signify the process of life from birth to the perfection of training: the stage of unconsciousness of the first seven days after birth; the stage of laughing and crying, around one year; the stage of determining to walk; the stage of walking; the stage of learning; the stage of religious practice as a homeless mendicant; the stage of enlightenment; and the stage of perfection and seclusion. The organs are those of sensation and procreation, such as eyes, ears, nose, womb, and testicles. Whereas Buddhism and Jainism commonly taught six or ten types of organ, Gosāla proposed two thousand, though we have no knowledge of what he meant.

5. *Shoki Girishia Tetsugaku Dampenshū* (Collection of fragments of early Greek philosophy), trans. and ed. Mitsuo Yamamoto (Tokyo: Iwanami Shoten, 1958), 15.

6. Ibid., 63.

7. Herodotus, *The Histories,* bk. 2, par. 123, rev. ed., trans. Aubrey de Sélincourt (New York: Penguin Books, 1972), 178.

8. *Milinda's Questions,* vol. 1, trans. I. B. Horner, vol. 22 of Sacred Books of the Buddhists (London: Luzac and Company, 1969), 55–56.

9. *Arrian: History of Alexander and Indica,* vol. 2, bk. 8, trans. E. Iliff Robson, The Loeb Classical Library (London: William Heinemann Ltd, 1933), 307.

10. *Commentary on the Great Perfection of Wisdom Sūtra,* vol. 17, pp. 186b–c.

11. The "small self" in Buddhism corresponds to the layperson's con-

ception of the self, as an entity different from other selves and from the universe. The "great self" is the self that is identified with the universe.

12. This philosophy is open to misconception, as is evidenced by the way Hirata Atsutane (Shinto theologian and nativist scholar, 1776–1843) interpreted it. The concept of the abode of neither thought nor non-thought was said to have originally been the teaching of Āḷāra Kālāma to Śākyamuni, who criticized that stance. Defending Āḷāra, Atsutane developed an argument based on misconception or even deliberate distortion. He interpreted "neither thought" as "not thinking of anything evil," and "neither non-thought" as "not not-thinking of good," that is, "thinking of good." He then said that thinking good and not thinking bad is liberation. Consequently he approved Āḷāra's teaching. Śākyamuni, he said, had angrily denounced Āḷāra's theory, because he, Śākyamuni, was an evil person who for the sake of his own liberation had abandoned parents, wife, and child. The discussion of the abode of neither thought nor non-thought as it appears in the Buddhist sūtras refers, of course, to a dimension transcending both good and evil.

13. *Vimalakīrti Sūtra,* ch. 9, "Entry into the doctrine of non-duality," *Taishō Tripiṭaka,* vol. 14, no. 475, p. 551c.

14. *Bṛhadāraṇyaka-upaniṣad,* ch. 4, section 5, subsection15.

Chapter 4

1. *Abhidharmakośa,* line 13, p. 57b.

2. For example, *Long Discourses,* fasc. 18, *Taishō Tripiṭaka,* vol. 1, pp. 114b–17c, and *Great Commentary,* fasc. 134, vol. 27, pp. 692b–96c.

3. Ibid., line 18, p. 62a.

4. *Great Commentary,* p. 701b.

5. *Abhidharmakośa,* line 20, p. 59a.

6. The *Great Commentary* says, "On the eighth day of the bright half of the month of Kārttika, day and night each last 15 *muhūrta* [periods of 48 minutes]. After this the days lessen and the nights lengthen in turn by one *lava* [1 minute and 36 seconds, the 900th part of a day and a night]. On the eighth day of the bright half of the month of Vaiśākha, day and night each last 15 [*muhūrta*]. After this the nights lessen and the days lengthen in turn by one *lava*" (p. 701c).

"The eighth day of the bright half of the month of Kārttika" clearly refers to the autumn equinox. Additionally, the statement that "the days lessen and the nights lengthen in turn by one *lava*" obviously corresponds to expressions in the *Abhidharmakośa* that "the days shorten," "the nights lengthen," and "[they] become shorter in turn by one *lava*." Therefore, the expression in the *Abhidharmakośa* that "the nights lengthen" most likely refers to a phenomenon associated with the autumn equinox.

However, according to the *Great Commentary*, the phenomenon of lengthening nights begins in the eighth month, Kārttika, while according to the *Abhidharmakośa* it occurs in the sixth month, Bhādrapada. How should we reconcile this seeming discrepancy?

One conceivable explanation is that over some two thousand years the time of the autumn equinox moves one month. The *Great Commentary* was composed around the second century C.E. and may have employed the old calendar. The *Abhidharmakośa,* however, was composed in the fifth century and could have been referring to the new calendar, which had by then come into use. The calendar of the *Vedas*, which had been used since around 1,500 B.C.E., remained influential for a long period of time. According to this calendar, the second month, Vaiśākha, was the month of the spring equinox. According to the new calendar, however, the spring equinox fell in the first month, Caitra. It is natural that over two thousand years a month's discrepancy had grown up.

As a matter of fact, the *Abhidharmakośa* lists the names of the months of the year beginning with Caitra, proof that it employed the new calendar. However, by this token, the autumn equinox should have fallen in the seventh month, Aśvayuja. This would be only one month before the eighth month, Kārttika, in which the equinox of the *Great Commentary*'s calendar fell. Why then was it said to have occurred two months earlier, in the sixth, Bhādrapada? In neither the old nor the new calendar does the sixth month contain either of the equinoxes or the solstices. Is there perhaps an error in the *Abhidharmakośa*?

The expression "the nights lengthen" appears as *vardhate niśā* in Sanskrit. "Shorten" is *hīyate.* These expressions do not appear to connote relative length; they merely mean "increase" and "decrease." Consequently the phenomenon of "lengthening nights" can certainly be connected with the summer solstice instead of with the autumn equinox. In India the words *uttarāyana* ("proceeding northward") and *dakṣiṇāyana* ("proceeding southward") are used to refer to the half-year periods, and indicate the time between the winter solstice and the summer solstice, and the summer solstice and the winter solstice, respectively. It should not be odd therefore to find other explanations of time based on the solstices. Furthermore, the Indic original of the *Great Commentary* has not been found; it is extant only in Chinese.

There is also a problem with the comparison of the Indian and Chinese (T'ang) calendars given in the *Records of the Western Regions of the Great T'ang Dynasty*. According to *Meiji-zen Nihon Tenmongaku Shi* (A history of Japanese astronomy before the Meiji period, ed. by Meiji-zen Nihon Kagakushi Kankōkai [Tokyo: Nihon Gakujutsu Shinkōkai, 1960], p. 23), "the month incorporating the autumn equinox is the eighth of the Chinese [T'ang] calendar," which should correspond to September of the Gregorian calendar (the month of the autumn equinox). Therefore the "seventh month" of the *Records of the Western Regions* is one month off.

7. The realms that undergo the cycle through one great *kalpa* are the first Dhyāna heavens. The First Dhyāna heavens consist of the three realms: Mahābrahmā, Brahma-purohita, and Brahma-kāyika. Their respective life spans are 1.5, 1.0, and 0.5 of a great *kalpa* (see figure 17). Since a great *kalpa* consists of eighty intermediate *kalpas,* half a great *kalpa* would therefore be forty intermediate *kalpas.* Thus the life spans can be calculated as sixty, forty, and twenty intermediate *kalpas,* respectively. By the same reasoning, the life span of the Mahābrahmā heaven lasts the cycles of creation, duration, and dissolution, that of the Brahma-purohita heaven lasts the cycles of duration and dissolution, and that of the Brahma-kāyika heaven lasts the cycle of dissolution.

8. *Sūtra of the Auspicious Kalpa, Taishō Tripiṭaka,* vol. 14, p. 1f.

9. They are the *Sūtra of the Names of One Thousand Buddhas in the Past Kalpa of Adornment* (*Taishō Tripiṭaka,* vol. 14, no. 446), the *Sūtra of the Names of One Thousand Buddhas in the Present Auspicious Kalpa* (Ibid., no. 447) and the *Sūtra of the Names of One Thousand Buddhas in the Future Kalpa of Constellations* (Ibid., no. 448). They are collectively called the "Sūtras of the Names of Three Thousand Buddhas."

10. Mochizuki, *Bukkyō Dai Jiten,* vol. 1, 940c.

11. Recently, when I had occasion to look up the entry on the Bodhisattva Maitreya in Mochizuki's *Bukkyō Dai Jiten,* I was brought up by the sight of the figure of 5,<u>76</u>0,000,000 (not 5,<u>67</u>0,000,000), given as the number of years between the death of Śākyamuni and the de-

scent of Maitreya as the new Buddha. In the Japanese edition of this work, *Shumisen to gokuraku* (Tokyo: Kodansha, 1973, p. 119), I had quoted a figure: "His [Maitreya's] appearance will be 5,670,000,000 years after the death of Śākyamuni." Not once since I wrote the figure had I any occasion to doubt it.

I wondered if Mochizuki's figure was a misprint. A quick review of over two dozen dictionaries and encyclopedias confirmed my figure. But, since Mochizuki's dictionary is one of the most authoritative of all Buddhist dictionaries, I still had doubts. I then consulted numerous sūtras in the *Taishō Tripiṭaka.* Many sūtras stated only that Maitreya's descent would occur "when the human life span reaches 84,000 years," or "when the human life span is 80,000 years." Virtually none say "after 5,760,000,000 years" or "after 5,670,000,000 years." All I found was the expression "5,670,000,000 years" in the *Sūtra of the Abode in the Womb* (P'u-sa ch'u-t'ai-ching), Fo-neng's Chinese translation (*Taishō Tripiṭaka,* vol. 12, no. 384, p. 1025c) and "5,600,000,000 years" in very few other sūtras.

Another statement in Mochizuki's entry is more revealing, however: "Maitreya's descent as the Buddha will occur after he has spent 4,000 years in the Tuṣita heaven; that is, in human terms, after 5,760,000,000 years." It is thought that Maitreya, receiving Śākyamuni's prediction that he would descend to earth in the future and attain buddhahood, went immediately to the Tuṣita heaven to await his future descent. (The choice of the Tuṣita heaven seems to be based on the tradition that Śākyamuni himself descended from that heaven.) Śākyamuni made no statements about when precisely in the future Maitreya would descend. It is not surprising, therefore, that people extrapolated from the 4,000-year life span of the Tuṣita heaven. We do not know if Maitreya is supposed to descend before or after completing his life span, but the latter would be the natural supposition. In my calculations in figure 17, I had figured the life span of the inhabitants of the Tuṣita heaven as 4,000 x [400 x (30 x 12)]. This was derived from the statement in Hsüan-tsang's Chinese translation of the *Abhidharma-kośa* (no. 1558, p. 61b) that "one day in the Tuṣita heaven is equivalent to 400 years in the human realm; the inhabitants of the Tuṣita heaven have a life span of 4,000 of those years," and assumed that a year in the Tuṣita heaven was made up of 360 days (12 months x 30 days), like that of the human realm. The result is 576,000,000, one decimal place smaller than Mochizuki's figure of 5,760,000,000, but with the same numerical sequence of 5, 7 and 6. Checking my calculations, I was astounded, and assailed with misgivings. Had I perhaps come to the hasty conclusion that the numerical sequence was consecutive, that is, 5, 6, and 7?

The Buddhist scholar Shōkō Watanabe has one theory about the order of these numbers. He states: "Taking one year to have 360 days and taking the life span of beings in the Tuṣita heaven to be 4,000 years, we arrive at a figure of 400 x 360 x 4,000 which equals 576,000,000 (referring to the *Sūtra of the Wise and the Fool* [Hsien-yü-ching], fasc. 12 [*Taishō Tripiṭaka,* vol. 4, no. 202, p. 437a]). But the figure began to be read as 5,760,000,000. In time the figures 7 and 6 changed places, probably because it was easier to say" (*Ai to Heiwa no Shōchō—Miroku-kyō* [The Maitreya sūtras: The symbol of love and peace], vol. 8 of *Nihonjin no Bukkyō* [Buddhism in Japan][Tokyo: Chikuma Shobō, 1966], 263–64).

The literary critic Kōichi Isoda puts forth another explanation (personal communication). He suggests that the figures 576 and 567 represent the difference between calculating the year at 360 days and 354 days, respectively. The *Abhidharmakośa,* in fact, says that six months of the year have thirty days and the other six months have twenty-nine days. This would give 354 days in the year, making the life span of the Tuṣita heaven 4,000 x 400 x 354 = 566,400,000, which could be rounded down to 566,000,000 or up to 567,000,000.

Another concern is that Mochizuki's figure of 5,760,000,000 years is larger than mine by one decimal place. Perhaps it reflects a calculation error on the part of ancient Indian scholars. Alternatively, there may have been separate traditions, which held that one day in the Tuṣita heaven was equivalent to 4,000 years in the human realm (not 400), or that the life span of the inhabitants of the Tuṣita heaven was 40,000 years (not 4,000 years). Isoda points out that sometimes the character for 100,000,000 is represented by the compound "thousand-ten thousand" (i.e., 10,000,000), by means of which the period under discussion would become 5,706,000,000. He also explains that 1,000,000 was later changed to 10,000,000.

According to the *Great Commentary,* "Certain people say: The amount of the life span of an inhabitant of the Tuṣita heaven is the same [as the] period [in which] the bodhisattva attains buddhahood, and the people of Jambudvīpa become mature enough to see the works of the Buddha. That is, when human beings have passed 57 *koṭis* [*koṭi* = 10,000,000] and 60 thousand years, the roots of goodness for instruction and being instructed are mature; and this is none other than the amount of the life span of an inhabitant of the Tuṣita heaven" (no. 1545, 892c). The expression 57 *koṭis* and 60 thousand years has undoubtedly dropped a hundred somewhere. In the *Great Commentary* (no. 1545, 698b), we find 57 *koṭis* and 60 *hundred* thousand years. We therefore arrive at the number 57 x 10,000,000 + 60 x 100 x 1000, which gives 576,000,000.

It is very likely that the number represented by "57 *koṭis* and 60 hundred thousand years" was expressed in the original Sanskrit as *saptapañcāśat-koṭayaḥ ṣaṣṭiśata-sahasrāṇi ca varṣāḥ. Saptapañcāśat* means 57. *Koṭayaḥ* is the plural form of *koṭi. Ṣaṣṭi* is 60, *śata* is 100, *sahasrāṇi* is 1,000 (plural). *Ca* means "and," and *varṣāḥ*, "years." Hsüan-tsang obviously tried to retain the flavor of the original in his translation (the *Great Commentary*), thus translating it literally as 57 *koṭis* and 60 *hundred* thousand years.

Concerning the Indian use of numerical degree, all sources agree in terms of units, hundreds and thousands, but after that there is considerable discrepancy. All the same, *koṭi* is fairly standard in usage and generally denotes the eighth degree (10,000,000). Therefore "57 *koṭis* and 60 hundred thousand years" would today be read as 576,000,000 and so Maitreya is to appear, neither 5,670,000,000 years nor 5,760,000,000 years, but 576,000,000 years after Śākyamuni's death.

The extra numerical place appears as a result of the way *koṭi* was interpreted in China and Japan. In Mochizuki's dictionary, *koṭi* is defined, based on the *Commentary on the Great Perfection of Wisdom Sūtra* (p. 87a), as 100,000,000, and no doubt it was this figure that became the base for interpreting 57 *koṭis* as 5,700,000,000. The 6 in the next line of degree should represent 6,000,000, but misinterpretation by subsequent scholars perhaps led to it being understood as 60,000,000, resulting in the figure of 5,760,000,000.

Chapter 5

1. *Perfection of Wisdom Sūtra in 25,000 Verses* (Fang-kuang pan-jo-ching), Wu-ch'a-lo's Chinese translation of the *Pañcaviṃśatisāhasrikā-prajñā-pāramitā, Taishō Tripiṭaka,* vol. 8, no. 221, p. 2a.

2. *Amitābha-sūtra* (A-mi-t'o-ching), Kumārajīva's Chinese translation of the *Smaller Sukhāvatī-vyūha, Taishō Tripiṭaka,* vol. 12, no. 366, p. 348a.

3. The term *śata-sahasra-koṭi-nayuta* appears in the Sanskrit text of the *Sūtra of Infinite Life* (Larger Sukhāvatī-vyūha), and the term *śata-sahasra-koṭi* appears in the *Amitābha-sūtra* (Smaller Sukhāvatī-vyūha). *Śata-sahasra* means "10 times 1,000." One would assume, then that *koṭi-nayuta,* or *koṭi,* means "one hundred million," but actually *koṭi* means "ten million," and *nayuta,* "ten thousand times greater." The Chinese word now used as "one hundred million" in ancient times meant "one hundred thousand," and in non-Buddhist usage the Indian *nayuta* is "one million." Whatever variation we may consider, we cannot reconcile the Indian number with the Chinese. It is possible the Chinese chose a phrase that was then in common usage to express the highest possible number.

4. Iwamoto, *Gokuraku to Jigoku,* 114.

5. Ibid., 116.

6. Ibid., 117.

7. Homer, *The Odyssey,* bk. 4, rev. ed., trans. E. V. Rieu (London: Penguin Books, 1991), 61.

8. See *Olympian Odes* 2:61–84 (*The Odes of Pindar,* trans. C. M. Bowra [Harmondsworth, England: Penguin Books, 1969], 82, 83) and *Dirges* 129–30. Shigeichi Kure, *Girishia Shinwa* (Greek mythology) (Tokyo: Shinchōsha, 1969), 200.

9. M. P. Nilsson, *The Minoan-Mycenaean Religion and Its Survivals in Greek Religion,* 2d ed. (Lund: Gleerup, 1950), 627.

10. M. G. Maspéro, "Étude sur quelques peintures et sur quelques textes relatifs aux funérailles," *Journal Asiatique,* ser. 7, tome 15 (1880): 150.

11. André Maricq, "La Grande Inscription de Kaniṣka et l'Étéo-Tokharien l'Ancienne Langue de la Bactriane," *Journal Asiatique,* 1958, pp. 378ff.

12. Benjamin Rowland, Jr., *Ancient Art of Afghanistan* (New York: Asia Society, 1966), 211.

Chapter 6

1. "It is a fact that in this country when a child is born they anoint him once a week with oil of sesame, and this makes him grow much

darker than when he was born. For I assure you that the darkest man is here the most highly esteemed and considered better than the others who are not so dark. Let me add that in very truth these people portray and depict their gods and their idols black and their devils white as snow. For they say that God and all the saints are black and the devils are all white. That is why they portray them as I have described. And similarly they make the images of their idols all black" (*The Travels of Marco Polo,* trans. Ronald Latham [Harmondsworth, England: Penguin Books, 1958], 277).

2. One day five hundred merchants, including one very wise man, found themselves wrecked on the shores of Sri Lanka. Very soon they were welcomed by five hundred gaily dressed *rākṣasa* women, and the men, overjoyed, went with them to their palace. So pleasant was palace life that the men forgot the passing of days, and eventually children were born of unions between the *rākṣasas* and the men. Each of the five hundred couples had a child. One day the wise leader of the merchants found himself in a strange part of the island and spied in the distance a castle, from which came the sound of voices raised in misery. He climbed a tree standing near the castle walls and saw before him a cruel sight. Several men were wailing, blue-faced, and a number of bones and blood surrounded them. He was told by one of them that they had once been shipwrecked also, and then were treated kindly. When the five hundred merchants arrived, though, the earlier men had been locked up in this castle and eaten one by one. "When new men arrive, you will meet the same fate," his informer warned. The merchant hurried back to tell his companions, and they all prayed for deliverance. Thereupon a horse alighted from heaven, and they all clambered onto it, some clinging to its tail, others to its legs. As the heavenly steed flew away, the *rākṣasa* women pursued it, saying how much they loved the merchants and reminding them of the children they had had together. Enticed by the promise of the pleasant life they could continue living together, all the merchants except the leader remained behind. The leader arrived safely back in India. The *rākṣasa* queen, his former spouse, was derided by the others for her husbandless state, and so she set out with her child and flew to the Indian mainland, reaching the parental home of the merchants' leader before the leader himself did. To the parents she presented herself as their son's wife, and her child as their grandchild, and then settled down to

await her husband's homecoming. When he arrived, he repudiated her, knowing the nature of her true form. The *rākṣasa* queen appealed to the Indian king, who wanted to punish the merchant, but he himself fell in love with the *rākṣasa* woman and made her his queen. Though the merchant warned the king, he was ignored, and that very night the king and his retainers were all devoured. The *rākṣasa* queen then flew back to Sri Lanka. Deprived of their ruler, the people of India began to search for a new king, and finally decided upon the merchant, because of his reputation for wisdom. The new king then led his army to Sri Lanka to attack the *rākṣasas*. Having subjugated them, he led his companions home.

3. Herodotus, *The Histories,* bk. 3, pp. 219, 245–46.

4. The Hindu temples at Khajurāho in central India are famous for their wealth of sculptural ornamentation. Distinctive among the sculptural subjects are figures in sexual embrace, even on the outer walls. Scenes of sexual activity include one man with several women, people copulating with animals, and men and women in complicated sexual acts. Such sexually explicit Tantrism seems to have occurred also in Japan within the clandestine Tachikawa branch of the Shingon sect.

Chapter 7

1. Nevertheless, the stūpa served as a kind of temple for those who came to worship the holy relics, a temple in which the Buddha dwelt. P. Mus equates the Buddha with the stūpa because both the Buddha and the stūpa were considered to be the cosmos (P. Mus, "Barabudur, les origines du stūpa," 618). M. Bénisti calls a stūpa with a figure of the Buddha portrayed on its outer surface, such as that shown in photo 4, a "stūpa with the Buddha affixed"(M. Bénisti, "Étude sur le stūpa dans l'Inde ancienne," *Bulletin de l'École Française d'Extrême-Orient,* tome 50, fasc. 1 [1960]: 81).

2. *Flower Garland Sūtra,* 80 fascs., chapter on the Lotus Repository World, Śikṣānanda's Chinese translation of 695–99, *Taishō Tripiṭaka,* vol. 10, no. 279.

3. There is mention of a lotus flower brought forth from each of the fragrant oceans in the center and in the east, and a world system rests on each of these lotus flowers. This structure does not agree with that of an actual lotus flower.

4. *Chāndogya-upaniṣad, Prapāṭhaka* (chapter) 6: *Khaṇḍa* (section) 12. Cf. *The Upanishads,* trans. F. Max Müller, vol. 1 of Sacred Books of the East (first published by Clarendon Press, 1879. Reprinted by Motilal Banarsidass, Delhi, 1965).

5. Joanna Williams, "The iconography of Khotanese painting," *East and West,* new series, vol. 23, nos. 1–2 (1973), 117.

6. One of these is Shashi Bhushan Dasgupta, *An Introduction to Tantric Buddhism,* 3d ed. (Calcutta: University of Calcutta, 1974).

Chapter 8

1. When Yama still resided in the heavenly realm, he owned two black-spotted dogs that led the dead safely to paradise. It seems that when Yama grew ferocious in aspect, his retainers followed suit. Thus the dogs (or possibly, their descendants) now tore off the limbs of those suffering in the hells (see pages 46, 52).

2. Cf. *The Zend-Avesta,* part 3, trans. L. H. Mills, vol. 31 of Sacred Books of the East (Delhi: Motilal Banarsidass, 1965 [1887]), p. 48.

3. Homer, *The Odyssey,* bk. 11, 176.

4. Another clue to the possible origin of Sanzu no kawa is the expression "three roads or ways" (*santo* in Japanese), which is found in literary sources much earlier than Sanzu no kawa. Saṃghavarman's Chinese translation of the Larger Sukhāvatī-vyūha (ca. 2d century) contains the compound "the suffering of the three roads," and the Sūtra of the Auspicious Kalpa (Hsien-chieh-ching, ca. 3d century) has "drowning in the three roads and the five destinations" (Sūtra of the Auspicious Kalpa, Dharmarakṣa's Chinese translation, *Taishō Tripiṭaka,* vol. 14, no. 425, 1–66). Did the "three roads" become Sanzu no kawa? The T'ang period lexicographer Hsüan-ying, in his *Dictionary of Pronunciations and Meanings of Words and Phrases in the Tripiṭaka* ([I-ch'ieh-ching-yin-i], *Koryo Tripiṭaka,* vol. 35 [Tokyo: Midori Sōgyō Company, 1974], p.171), defined the "three roads" as follows: "The 'three roads' borrows from the expression 'there are dangerous places of the three roads' found in the *Spring and Autumn Annals.* The character employed for 'road' is virtually identical in meaning to the more commonly used *tao.* It does not have the meaning of 'mire [written with the same character as "road"] and coal' [i.e., 'great misery']. In Sanskrit works it is called *āpanna-gati,* which in Chinese translation is 'the unfortunate realms of rebirth [hells, hungry spirits, animals].'"

This explanation makes it apparent that there is no element in "three roads" that has any connection with a river, or any direct relation to the idea of suffering. Neither is there any such relationship with a river in the concept of *āpanna-gati*. Furthermore, the Sanskrit version of the *Larger Sukhāvatī-vyūha* does not contain any expression identical to "the suffering of the three roads," and does not depict any river. The meaning of the term may be one of the following: (1) A steep mountain in China, located in the southwestern part of Lo-yang and north of I-shui; (2) hell, hungry spirits, animals; or (3) the road of fire (the hells), the road of blood (animals), the road of swords (hungry spirits). There is nothing here that could have developed into the idea of Sanzu no kawa.

Mochizuki's dictionary (vol. 2, p. 1621b) states that the *sanzu* of Sanzu no kawa was originally written not with characters meaning "three ways" but with characters denoting "to bury" and "head." One has the strong impression that this compound is a transliteration of a foreign word; it hardly seems likely that it means "to bury a head." One theory proposes that the compound meaning "three ways" was used first and that the meaning "to bury a head" came later, as a distortion or pun. This is hard to believe; there seems to be no reason for changing the first compound into the second. We do not know, either, what word the second compound was used to transliterate. Neither *Styx* nor *haētu* ("shore") fits, though *setu,* the Indic form of *haētu,* bears some phonetic resemblance to *sanzu* (ancient *sandu*). It is difficult, however, to trace this connection in literary sources.

5. Mochizuki, *Bukkyō Dai Jiten,* vol. 2, 1621.

6. According to the *Yin-kung* of the *Ch'un-ch'iu tso-chuan* (Tso's commentary on the Spring and Autumn Annals) (Tadashi Kamata, *Shunjū sashiden,* vol. 30 of *Shinshaku kambun taikei* [Tokyo: Meiji Shoin, 1971], pp. 48–54), Duke Wu (r. 770–44 B.C.E.) of Cheng (a state under the Chou dynasty, occupying the present district of K'ai-feng in Honan) married Wu-chiang. Wu-chiang gave birth to the future Duke Chuang (r. 743–01), who was a breech birth. Because of his irregular birth, Wu-chiang came to have an aversion for her eldest child and favored her second son Kung-shu Tuan, desiring that he succeed to the dukedom. She often pressed her husband to make him his heir but he would not.

When Chuang inherited his father's position, Wu-chiang incited Kung-shu Tuan to rebel, but the new duke quelled the rebellion and banished his brother. Then he imprisoned his mother at a place called Ch'eng-ying and vowed to her that he would never set eyes on her again until he met her in the Yellow Springs (Hades) on death.

Soon, however, he repented of his attitude. At that time a border guard from Ying-ku called Ying K'ao-shu heard about Duke Chuang and sent tribute to him, wanting to meet him. The Duke invited him to dinner. Ying, however, did not eat the specially prepared meat. When the Duke asked the reason, he replied, "I have a mother. She always eats what I do. My mother has never had such excellent food, so I intend to take the meat home and give it to her to eat." The Duke said, "It is good that you have a mother to whom you can give delicious things to eat. Ah, I alone have no mother!" The Duke explained what had happened and felt a sharp pang of sorrow and remorse. Then Ying said to him, "If that is so, you need have no grief. If you dig a hole in the ground and keep digging until a well begins to flow, and then meet, mother and child, beside the underground well of water [the subterranean Yellow Springs], no one will be able to say that the duke broke his vow." The Duke carried out the plan to the letter. After that, mother and son maintained a good relationship.

7. See the *Classified and Annotated Legal Codes of the Three Eras* (compiled 1002–1089) (Shintō taikei—koten hen: Ruijū sandaikyaku [Shintō system on Classics: Ruijū sandaikyaku], ed. Shintō Taikei Hensankai [Tokyo: Shintō Taikei Hensankai, 1993], pp. 339–40) and the *Veritable Record of Three Generations of Japan* (Sandai jitsuroku, ed. Ariyoshi Saeki, vol. 8 of *Rikkokushi* [Tokyo: Asahi shimbunsha, 1930], p. 472).

8. Mochizuki, *Bukkyō Dai Jiten*, vol. 2, p. 1422c–1423a.

Chapter 9

1. *Zōtei Kumazawa Banzan* (Kumazawa Banzan, enlarged edition), ed. Sumio Taniguchi and Michio Miyazaki (Tokyo: Meicho Shuppan, 1980), 161.

2. Saigyō, *Saigyō: Poems of a Mountain Home*, trans. Burton Watson (New York: Columbia University Press, 1991), 40.

Index

Acknowledgments

This book is a translation of *Shumisen to Gokuraku* published by Kodansha, Tokyo, 1973. The following essays by the same author, originally published in Japanese, were incorporated into this book and are published with the permission of the original publishers.

Pages 42 through 47 of chapter 2 are excerpts from the May 25, June 5, and June 25, 1976, issues of *Sanzō-shū* (Collection of the Tripiṭaka), published by Daitō Shuppan, Tokyo.

Note 11 of chapter 4 is an excerpt from the September and October 1980 issues of *Shunjū* (Spring and autumn), published by Shunjū-sha, Tokyo.

Chapter 6, "Buddhist Deities," and Appendix: "Linear Measurement" are from *Bukkyō ni Miru Sekai-kan* (The worldview seen in Buddhism), published by Daisan Bummei-sha, Tokyo, 1980.

Chapter 7, "The Buddha and the Cosmos," is taken from *Ajia no Uchū-kan* (Asian views of the universe), edited by Kōhei Sugiura and Kenji Iwata and published by Kodansha, Tokyo, 1988.